The Godseeker's Guide

The Godseeker's Guide

Rabbi Lionel Blue

continuum

Published by the Continuum International Publishing Group
The Tower Building, 11 York Road, London SE1 7NX
80 Maiden Lane, Suite 704, New York, NY 10038

www.continuumbooks.com

First published 2010
Reprinted 2010

British Library Cataloguing-in-Publication Data
A catalogue record for this book is available from the British Library.

ISBN 978-1847-06418-9

Typeset by Kenneth Burnley, Wirral, Cheshire
Printed and bound in Great Britain

Contents

Introduction

This book was not written in a library or study but mostly on tops of buses, deep in London's Underground, in cafés, while waiting in hospitals, in the studios of the BBC and in hospitable places of worship where I could shelter from the rain – in the places where heaven suddenly happened to me.

It is not possible to programme religious experiences exactly – they are like the intuitions of lyrics and the stabbing insights encountered in psychoanalysis. On this level, there's a lot of 'as if' stuff.

I began with my hesitant but increasing trust in my own religious experience and that of others who I have known and trusted – neither uncritically – who have passed on tips and helps for the journey.

I hope the halting progress I've described may be of use to others on a similar journey also trying to get to heaven – taking one step forwards, and half a step backwards – like me.

I thank Heather who prepared and edited this book, and Hilary who brought order out of chaos. And Jim, Henk and John, Theo, Wendy, Guy and Marc for their encouragement.

And special thanks to Grey College of the University of Durham, its Master, Professor Martyn Chamberlain and his wife Sarah, Henry Dyson, the Senior Common Room, students and staff who, together, gave me the precious gift of a second education in my third age.

Chapter 1

The Purpose of this Book

Dear Godseeker!

This book is what the title says – a help, a companion, a discursive personal handbook if you are on a God search, or thinking about one, or preparing to go on one. It is not an exhaustive set of instructions, nor a detailed route map or timetable for your own journey to heaven. The path to the divine is stranger than that, with more surprises, twists and wrong turnings that turn out to be right turnings, and vice versa, than you ever bargained for when you started out.

Nor is this book an attempt to sell you any particular form or image of God, or whether the mystery is a He, She, or It. My own limitations will undoubtedly creep in to everything I say. I cannot stand outside my own self and life experience, or the experience of those Godseekers I have known – alive or dead. Discount them when and if they get obtrusive. It isn't possible to be objective about the path to love and enlightenment. We are all, as my one-time prophet Marx said, 'conditioned' by our environment; though not 'determined' by it, as he so rightly added.

But more connects us than we realize, despite our different faiths, creeds, doubts and needs. We are all gazing at the same reality in the centre of a circle, but from different points on that circle's circumference. Yes, we are looking at the same point, but from different, or seemingly opposite, directions. Remember this when you are inclined to indulge in knock-about religious arguments! They can be fun and let off steam, but where do they get you? Don't let them get you angry!

Hopefully this book will give you useful information, tips or insights to help you on your own journey. Some of the information will always need updating as the scene is constantly changing. New spiritual movements come in just as old retreat centres close up and change addresses or contact numbers. The reality might not change, but our perception of it does and is responsive to fashion like anything else. The writer is well aware that 'of making many books there is no end' as Ecclesiastes said, 'and much study can be a weariness of the flesh' – though he has not felt this while Godseeking. This book was meant to answer a need – honestly if not always correctly or wisely – but of that, dear Godseeker, you must be the judge.

I do not know why I have written of 'the writer' so portentously in the third person (speaking of God tends to inflate the ego). The writer is me, Lionel Blue, a Reform rabbi, who teaches in seminaries and from pulpits and speaks on the radio, and who, to his own surprise and satisfaction, is an OBE and twice an honorary Doctor.

I determined on this book in a theatre dressing-room while waiting to go on stage for a one-man show. I was panicky, as usual. 'Would I remember the punch-lines of my jokes and stories?', 'Would there be five, fifty or five hundred in the audience?', 'Would I be a success?', 'Would the evening cover costs?'

'Believe in your own goods!' said a voice in me. It was that of my God guide – I call him Fred. 'Stop massaging your own ego, totting up and fussing about the plusses and minuses of everything and nothing. Trust Me!'

'OK,' I replied, relieved, 'just stick around and stay with me!'

Being an imaginative person, I located his presence in a chair beside me, as it were, and started to think about what the audience wanted or needed from me spiritually.

'Fred' grunted approval. To hell with success and the numbers game! We were all going on the same journey following different routes. I had to help them heavenwards, as they were helping me. We had been drawn together to pool our knowledge and experience: a company of people on a pilgrimage through life – a feeling which stayed with me throughout the show and afterwards, while signing books and flyers, or drinking together at the theatre bar.

I would do my bit by writing down my own experience to help us on this journey. Speaking to people through a microphone or a camera is a strange business. Sometimes you have to make contact with your listeners' actual flesh and blood to make sense. Which I suppose is why I have literally fallen off both a pulpit and a stage to express our developing spiritual intimacy. My bruises were worth it and convincing, although my then unknown epilepsy might have been responsible.

'OK, Rabbi Blue, you told them your truth, jawing your head off; how did they tell you theirs?' I've always insisted on leaving the theatre house lights full on, so that I could read the faces of the audience. How much spirituality did they want, and how much was relevant to their situation? How much sex and laughter did I need to help wash my metaphysics down? Their expressions told me.

My worry in the dressing-room was quite unnecessary, as Fred had said. As life has gone on, I've trusted him more and more. Which is reassuring, as I've just attained a not so healthy 80, and ageing, as you get near it or in it, is no joke.

'Help, Fred! Where are you?'

The names of God

I have not used a consistent name for God throughout this guide. It is a peculiar problem of my own creation, and you, dear God-seekers, might find it confusing. His names have changed and evolved as he and I have got to know each other better and, though I came to him out of need, those needs have changed, often turning inside out. I stayed with him because gradually I began to trust him, became fond of him, and found that the traditional formal names did not fit our relationship. From the military sounding Lord God of Hosts, he has become my guide into another dimension. What he is in himself remains a mystery; and I am content to leave it that way.

The medieval Jewish Mystics called God the Ayin, the Nothing in Hebrew (with a capital N) because he is No-thing, and the Nothing that we can ever understand. But that is a name I cannot use. The nearest I get on this path is the more affectionate Whomsoever-Whatsoever, which means to me Nothing that I can or will ever understand but can't live without. To the Mystics, God was the place where the opposites unified, which I can understand intellectually, but can't feel.

I can't use names such as The Eternal or The Almighty either, because they chill me, and it doesn't matter to me that much if he is All anything, being beyond space and time.

In my experience he is the lover I never quite found, the brother I never had, and the friend who has never let me down. The force that brings good out of evil or folly, and, more usefully, the strength of redemption in me, the little bit of the Messiah in me and in others, his image in my being which brings laughter out of poverty and persecution. So, when he's putting on the style, he's my Friend in High Places, and when we're chatting and holding hands, so to speak, he's Fred. Why Fred? I don't know! It's a friendly, unpretentious name, and that's how he appears to me, how he popped up in my imagination.

I also call him 'Lord' but understandably feminists are not happy with this. I could probably get used to calling him 'Lady' but this doesn't find much favour either. Sometimes I want to escape from using all human relationships and call him, as the Bible does so many times, 'Heaven', because this is how I know him. Heaven happens frequently in life, in small incidents. Sometimes we invoke it and sometimes it 'happens' as an act of grace, a free gift. Heaven is a strong word for me because I actually feel it pulling me towards it. Many Godseekers feel that this is true for them too and is the basis of their trust and belief.

I don't use parental images for God like Father or Mother. In my childhood my parents were a bit of a mis-match and, though united in their love for me, they each thought of me in very different ways. My father saw me as a future fighter, the Jewish hope in the boxing ring, and my mother thought of me as a legal tycoon with a platoon of secretaries. I did them both in the eye by becoming a rabbi, which my slower father understood better than my quicker, more intelligent mother. But I think it is unnecessary and an added confusion to project the private hang-ups of my family onto the cosmos.

Sometimes I think of God as a baby or a beggar, not as someone who can help me but whom I can help. He must get pretty upset looking at the world he created. A lot of it is quite monstrous!

My prayers have become simpler over the years. They're mainly 'Stick around, I need you' or 'I can't do without you', or 'How do I deal with this one?' or 'Let's hold hands!' or 'Thanks for showing me that!' or 'I love you!' Quite often we do hold hands and sit in companionable silence.

Two simple English hymns seem to express all my needs: my friend Sydney Carter's 'One more step . . .' and, when I get really lovey-dovey, 'All that I am, All that I do, All that I'll ever have I offer now to you'. I sing them to myself and begin to feel airborne or rather spirit-borne, and I change the words of both to fit my feelings at the time.

There is a Jewish mystical chant which goes 'du, du, du, du', which is why it is called a dudele – a 'you' song. 'You, you, you, you, you, always you, ever you, before me you, behind me you', etc., etc. I must admit I haven't yet sung it successfully like my other songs. I'm too earthbound a spirit, not on such a mystical level most of the time. Dear Godseeker, why don't you have a go? It's like hypnotic, mystical chewing gum. Effective though. A lot of elementary mysticism may seem childish but it isn't, it's childlike!

The wrong motives for the right reasons

Don't worry if the 'wrong' motives have set you Godseeking! Whatever they were at the beginning, they'll get purified en route.

So what made you begin your search in the first place? Perhaps you've tripped over a bit of transcendence somewhere somehow – you sheltered from the rain in a silent chapel and the silence wasn't as empty as you thought. Perhaps you're just schizoid or a natural ventriloquist or hypnotized by your own sermons. Perhaps you've been overwhelmed by the night sky – its size and splendour.

There are so many reasons for starting out on such a search. A broken love affair maybe, or the desolation of being stood up, or seeing the good and recognizing that it is alive and personal as well as beautiful. Perhaps to cure your own loneliness or emptiness, or trying to believe that you matter. Perhaps you want to mix with the right people, or at least be buried among them. Or maybe you want to manipulate the universe and this is as good a juju as any. Or you've suddenly fallen in love with a God that died on you as a kid, or you want a divine daddy and support in life. Have you been told that God can help alcoholics (he does – for some), or because you've fallen in love with Love, or with his or her attractive representative? You might need extra strength as a carer who can't cope, or extra courage (like I did) to get through a heavy analysis (yes, it did provide it), or perhaps your business has gone bust in a recession, and you interpret this as a divine sign to invest in another dimension. You just can't believe matter is eternal – neither can I! (It may not be as solid as it seems either – according to Quantum physicists.) Maybe you want to thank some Being somewhere for a joy you've experienced. Maybe you've discovered your soul. Perhaps you need a Big Brother or a friend you can really trust, a lover who won't walk out on you (and you won't walk out on her or him, which might be more to the point).

You can also catch God as you catch measles and get 'born again', to the consternation of your bewildered friends and family. Edith Stein, reading Teresa of Ávila, said, 'This is the truth!' She became a nun and ended up in a gas chamber. At Oxford, I met a student who read Thomas Aquinas and disappeared into a monastery. Such experiences often happen at university for a very good reason: you go up looking for wisdom and you get fobbed off with arid cleverness.

Lots of people go into the God business more light-heartedly. At the beginning they want to *use* God, which is fair enough. After all, most religions say that is just what God wants. Lots of people join synagogues or churches for that reason. They often want their children to be well and expensively educated in the same beliefs that they've jettisoned. But something sucks them too into the religious setup they have signed up to, and their attendance at committees and meetings goes up, and so does the telephone bill. They started out to use and misuse religion but now it begins to use them, and their original motives have matured or vanished or been transformed, to their own bewilderment. I went into religion because I was lonely and loveless – as a temporary stop-gap till I could get a real lover. Like them, I got more than I bargained for.

It can be the same with prayer: from Father Harry Williams I learned about two men who applied for the same job and met in the waiting-room for their interview. It was credit-crunch time and they were desperate. One prays simply, 'Oh God, let me get that job!'

Then he sees his rival, downcast and absorbed, certainly praying the same thing. Feeling uncomfortable, he then alters his prayer. 'Lord,' he says, 'let me get that job – if it be thy will.' But that too obvious get-out clause makes him feel worse than ever. He's now a hypocrite as well as heartless. 'God damn it,' he prays for the third time, 'do what you bloody well like!' An honest and honourable prayer indeed! His prayer has purified itself.

Pray that the same self-purifying process happens to the motives which start us on our religious search.

I think back to my motives for becoming a rabbi – for my 'call'. I had to set them out for a committee which could award me a scholarship. I gave a lot of good reasons, which were all true enough. I did feel a responsibility for the survivor Jewish communities in Europe. I did feel that the weight of a great tradition depended on me, etc., etc. But I did not mention that I liked listening to the sound of my own voice, that I was just coming out of analysis following a breakdown (which is why I got only a lower second), that my obliging girlfriend was not exactly my girlfriend, only my friend, that I was frightened of the business world, etc., etc. I also did not tell them that I had fallen in love with Love, which would have really put the cat among the pigeons. ('Mr Blue, you will understand, of course, that we need a psychiatric report . . .') I felt guilty about all that I didn't say. Until one day, in a silent empty Room of Prayer, I told Whomsoever, Whatsoever, Love, and my Friend Fred in High Places, all my jumbled motives and my wrong reasons for doing the right thing. And their burden dropped from my shoulders, as it did from Christian in Bunyan's *Pilgrim's Progress*, and I've never worried about them again.

The world is becoming a more and more uncertain place, what with terrorists and climate change and credit-crunch, with atom bombs for sale on the black market and the collapse of oh-so-solid banks. Will the Royal Family and God go the same way? God forbid!

Everything that until recently seemed so safe is now precarious. Augustine (St Paul?) knew this well: 'Here is no abiding city!' And old-time Jews still leave a corner of their rococo rooms unplastered to remember the transitory nature of the things of this world.

It doesn't matter much why you go into the God business – much more important is what happens to you while you're in it. Just accept your spiritual call and thank God for it.

'If a horse drops from heaven, don't examine its teeth,' said my grandfather. He was a wily one!

Problems

Hymie and Mo. 'You haven't yet asked me about my problems!' Hymie said accusingly. 'So sorry!' said Mo, penitently. 'How are your problems?' 'Don't ask!' Hymie said tearfully.

One of the best ways of taking off into the spirit is by having a problem – two or more even better. Not the political type concerning others which you can debate in halls or chatter about at parties, but a personal one concerning yourself. You're neurotic and you know it, or A loves B and B loves C who loves A, and you're poor B, piggy in the middle, or you dine alone at a table for one, on holiday among pairs and doubles, or you're a bright Jewish lad at university who peaked before his time, and your self-confidence has collapsed, or you're forced to realize early on that being an un-gay homosexual you're an outsider in an insider Jewish society. I am not going on with this dreary list. You get the point.

Don't curse your problem! For many of us, it's only when we're slipping and falling that we're finally reduced to praying – real praying, not reciting liturgy or listening to sad mood music from a choir! Crying out 'Help!' into the unknown emptiness may sound primitive, but it's basic and it works because it's honest. So something, someone, speaks up inside you or from far away, from another dimension of existence. You don't even have to know who you're calling on or praying to (I've used my him/her/it, my WW, my Whomsoever-Whatsoever and, eventually, I fell upon Fred which he/she/it seemed to like) and I was surprised when the beginnings of answers and understanding formed in a part of my mind I hadn't used much before.

You aren't alone. By chance, in the middle of my adolescent crisis time I opened the first page of John Bunyan's *Pilgrim's Progress* which I plucked from a bookshelf at a tedious student drinks party and was riveted by the opening words:

> *As I lay in a den in the wilderness of the world, I saw a man who cried out, 'What shall I do?'*

That was me over 60 years ago. For some people, it comes out of a 'morning after the night before' experience, as when Buddha walked gently over the snoring bodies forsaking his wealth and power and the wilderness of his world to meditate under the Bo tree. It can come after a night of easy sex when you wake up and look at your partner with loathing, not love, because you're ashamed or panicking – like Amnon in the Bible, for example.

What are the answers to such a banal and basic prayer? I've selected some examples from my own experience or from others whose honesty I trust.

Many experience the world in a new way. It's still the same world all right and there are no miracles or transformation scenes like those which end old-fashioned pantomimes, but you begin to see that world in a new light, with detachment or touched by love. For some it's accompanied by an out-of-body experience – I hasten to add 'as it were' – because miracles and pious vaudeville haven't figured so far in my life, though I'm open to them. The nearest I've got is that, while holding a sherry glass in one hand and a piece of asparagus in the other, and yacking away thirteen to the dozen at a large professional works party, at the BBC for example, a bit of me moves away and, from somewhere near the ceiling, looks down at our friendly toiling moiling mob with compassion. For a moment I've been pulled up by the silent invisible gravity of heaven into the spiritual dimension.

For those who've experienced this or something similar, the release from the ego for a while changes their lives. They want to give things up or away – their place in the checkout queue at the supermarket, for example. They chat to a beggar and give up not only their small change but a tiny bit of themselves.

This is one way, dear Godseeker, you begin to see a 'new heaven and a new earth'.

But to begin to visit this new dimension on a regular basis, even if only in very small doses, you may need a guide to this still unknown territory. Dante had Beatrice and Virgil to draw him on, and Christian in *Pilgrim's Progress* had his angel to give him courage. For some, myself included, this was the beginning of an inner conversation. I gradually became friendly with my own guide whom jokingly I called Fred as he took shape in my mind. Why Fred? It just felt right and he was and is my friend. Perhaps because friendship is the relationship I'm best at, with some very bad lapses, and Fred and friend sound alike.

Some modern prayer books talk about the Eternal or Source of Being, but that's too grand and heavy for me when I need him. I imagine him rather like the Jesus in Stanley Spencer's painting of the resurrection. He's no sad chestnut Aryan, but rough, fat and burly.

But more about Fred later – after I become a paid-up, practising Godseeker.

In the middle of my woes, I took courage and asked one of my teachers about my problems. He answered somewhat elliptically,

'Mr Blue, your successes will make you clever, but only your problems will make you wise.' It was no answer, but it was very true and it began to change my thinking about my problems, and I have stored away his remark in my private scripture.

Chapter 2

Why Did I Become a Godseeker?

Introduction

I forswore religion at the age of five and instead marched with my uncle's Reds because they were modern and non-miraculous. They too could prophesy, but scientifically; and they fed me with biscuits after processions and promised me that one day I could carry the Red banner.

Nevertheless I never gave up the memory of my grandmother's superstitious but real piety and the holy glow of her Sabbath candles that seemed to shine in me. I never told the comrades about my subversive secret but, looking back, I suspect that many of the Jewish comrades felt the same. Such things were unmentionable, like sex.

After my Bar Mitzvah, my Confirmation, I spoke into the emptiness of silent synagogues when no service or sermon was happening, and I listened for the echo of a voice. That too was a secret – like political porn in fact. It was my virtual reality, like my mother's Hollywood fantasies or the political fantasies of grandpa, a disciple of Kropotkin. The times were dark, and a little 'opium of the masses' did not come amiss.

Childhood pilgrimage

Dear Godseeker,

Later on I shall recommend and consider more formal pilgrimages. Here is an informal one I suggest to you at the beginning of this book – a bus journey to the house, flat or furnished rooms where you lived as a child, to consider and ponder your childhood religion, even if it was a hand-me-down from someone else's piety.

Until sex and success enter a child's life, there is often a remarkably straightforward experience of a spiritual dimension. I remember feeling puzzled and profound considering death when I was five, and the taste, smell and feel of goodness. Rudolph the Red-Nosed Reindeer, the miracle of the Chanukah lights and White Christmas; and the flood of religious kitsch was brought in by adults, not by me.

My early religion was mostly granny's. She looked after me while my mother was in hospital and my father tried to sell ice cream in winter – there was no other work for bespoke tailors after the slump of 1929–30 and the arrival of the 'Thirty Shilling Suit'. All I have left of her is a plate, a photograph imitating an oil painting, some saucy Yiddish stories, and the combination of cookery and kindness I learned watching her feed neighbours on the dole, the mad woman down the street, or beggars and striking miners – and all on pennies. Even the street where we lived has gone – a land-mine flattened it, and now council flats cover it like the pyramid over the Egyptian Pharaoh in the British Museum.

I recently made a private pilgrimage to a café near to where she used to live. I drank Russian tea in a glass as she did and meditated on her religion, because I'm now much older than she was (like most women of her generation she was prematurely worn out), and it was high time to work out once again the scripture of my own life. Granny might have preferred me to turn to traditional

Scriptures, but they are about 'them then', people long ago and far away, and I'm concerned with 'me now', and the two don't relate easily.

Though her belief was medieval and mine is modern like my ma's, granny was a shrewd cookie who would have understood that her world had changed beyond recognition. So miracles are a puzzle, and I'm wary of applying ancient customs to modern conditions. That way brings disaster and injustice, as we know from the news, for tradition contains both junk and treasure and is not the only way to God, though that was the only way granny knew.

I forsook granny's religion when I was five or six. She had told me that if I prayed for something with all my heart and if it wasn't just to benefit me but everybody, God would surely grant it. Well, I prayed fervently for the speedy demise of Adolph Hitler and Sir Oswald Mosley – but neither happened. Some weeks later, when I went to fetch granddad's *Daily Herald*, there was a picture of them both flourishing as the righteous are supposed to do – like the bay tree. So regretfully I had to face the uncomfortable fact that I was a modern, like my ma, and granny's juju (Jew-Jew) just didn't work. So I gave my uncle's juju a try, and marched with the Reds instead, who made much of me as I piped up 'Redfront, Redfront!' during the pauses, and rewarded me with cookies.

In the years ahead I tried dutifully to be an atheist. I certainly didn't believe in God and, if he did exist, I didn't like him. The Nazi world we were moving into was too wicked for that; and God's self-appointed representatives I didn't trust. But, because of granny, I did believe in 'good' and it was alive. I had witnessed it and felt it: it had lifted me into another world. I felt its beauty long after granny died, and I still occasionally lit the Sabbath candles like granny and whispered to it gabbling some words that sounded like Hebrew.

I did not understand holiness, of course, but I don't think anybody does. It is from a very strange dimension indeed – you either experience it or you don't. But the seeds of it were planted in me, and they surfaced and flowered much later in life, during a Quaker meeting which I crept into by chance to get out of the rain.

Dear Godseeker, that was the time I wandered into cold lecture halls advertised in the *New Statesman*. I sat in the back, munching toffees, listening to teachers and wise men and saints, some phoney, many self-hypnotized phonies, and a very few who set me aback because they knew that other dimension that my granny had introduced me to. I hoped I'd bump into a fresh revelation more solid than a few childhood memories of past piety which seemed too see-through and frail to bear the burden of my life.

A rabbi told me that after every disaster in Jewish history, a new revelation, a new 'book' had appeared which had turned our suffering into wisdom. So where was the book that would make sense of the Holocaust and Auschwitz and the Warsaw Ghetto, I asked him? He shook his head. He had no quick, slick reply, which made me respect him. Was something hidden happening, though we didn't see it? I thought about what he had said. Perhaps in a democratic age revelation doesn't come from mountaintops or high places heralded by trumpets and thunder and lightning, but democratically. If we all put together honestly the truths we've learned in life, like pieces in a jigsaw, God's presence would shine in it. It is there in the adolescent Anne Frank's diaries, in Etty Hillesum, in Titus Brandsma's poem in prison, and in so many others.

These are some of the truths I stumbled upon, none original but all personally tested, mostly from refugees:

*   'Your successes make you clever, Mr Blue, but your problems make you wise.'
*   'We need a religious home – not a religious prison.'
*   'Love people as they are, not as you want them to be.'

- 'If you trust and lean on nothing, that nothing will support you', and
- 'If your faith makes you kinder, more generous and more honest about yourself to yourself, you're on the right road.'

Granny would have said 'Amen' to that.

A last word about my teacher granny. Her saucy humour redeemed her piety from fanaticism because few fanatics laugh at themselves. So after Russian tea in the café and a memorial prayer she would have liked, I'll tell her this story and hear her cackle, as it were, in heaven. A refugee from Siberia to the West does so well he brings his poor granny over from the old country – she is awestruck by his possessions. Timidly she asks, 'Do you keep the kosher food laws my baby?' 'Sorry, gran, but I can't afford to be an outsider.' She tries again, 'Do you go to synagogue then?' 'No, I've got to go to too many company meetings.' After a silence she cries out piteously, wringing her hands, 'Tell me, tell me, my baby, are you still circumcised?'

Evacuated, I wandered into churches

In the poor Jewish East End of London, ecumenism (so favoured now) was a sin.

Before I was evacuated in 1939 I had never even entered a church. The rabbis warned against it, and more importantly, so did granny. A religious teacher told us improving stories to bolster our resolve. 'If you were chased by a snake in the desert,' he said, 'and you could only take refuge in a mosque or a church, which would you choose?' You were supposed to pick the former because the images made the latter dangerous and dicey. If you were especially pious of course you could try to placate the snake. I decided I would jump into the nearest shelter irrespective of creed or denomination. But of course I never uttered such advanced ecumenical views at religion classes.

After hearing this, we kids dared each other to peek into a church. I took two or three good peeks but the images were so frightening or sad, I gave up. I must have missed the crib, which I would have liked. Granny also tried to bolster my piety with improving stories. In a West End store a benign Santa Claus, handing out presents, asks a little boy, 'And how do you celebrate Christmas, little boy?' 'I don't,' answers the little boy self-righteously, 'I'm Jewish.' The eyes of Santa fill with tears which splash down his cheeks. 'A leb'n af dein kappele,' he says in Yiddish. 'A blessing on your head, my child!' When I asked if he still got a present, I was shut up for my materialist tendencies.

But it wasn't as simple as that. I thought the festival beautiful with the lights in London's Regent Street and the electric trains in Hamleys and White Horse Inn and, most beautiful of all, the transformation scenes at the pantomime. It was magic!

I couldn't have been that materialist because I wasn't envious. I had a girlfriend at the time called Alice. We were six or seven and unofficially engaged. We had met at the cut-price grocer's where our families sent us to buy broken biscuits, cracked eggs and yesterday's cakes. And looking into shop windows we played our virtual reality game.

'If I had a half-crown, Alice,' I'd say solemnly, 'I'd buy you that baby doll with the sleeping eyes.' 'And I'd buy you, Lionel, those building-blocks to make us a house,' she replied ardently. We stared at each other – overwhelmed by our unselfishness and generosity.

Everybody we knew played what we now call the virtual reality game; it sweetened the hardness of their lives. My mother and her sisters dreamed of dancing with Fred Astaire or held tight against Tarzan's massive chest. Grandpa dreamed of cut-price whisky for oldies. And my cousins dreamed of revolution and workers' rights. One of them read in a shop window the message of the angels and the left-wing lines in the Magnificat. 'They were as good as the Internationale,' he said, puzzled but approving.

I learned some very important lessons from commercial Christmases – that Christians could throw a religious party just like Jews and that, while the party lasted, people became very nice to each other, which meant a lot in our part of London – always liable to explode into tribal warfare for anything or nothing, especially at Easter time.

This attraction to Christmas good cheer even caused problems at high school, where many Jewish children, though not the true traditionalists of course, wanted to join in everything, which the headmaster rightly regarded as unsuitable. A compromise was cobbled together. Jewish children could join in the carol choir but not the Nativity Play. Some thought he was anti-Semitic but I thought he was more than fair. The trouble was that none of us knew any theology. It wasn't a rabbinic subject and I didn't even study it years later at my seminary. Religion for me was reading prayers in Hebrew, rituals and piety.

In any case theology would have been beyond our comprehension. All I knew about virgins, and it wasn't much, was that some poor but decent ugly girls can't grow out of it. So to get them married, a pious congregation collected dowries to make them a more attractive proposition. Not romantic but effective.

I never got the Messiah business straight. Granny said 'Az der Meshiach v't kimmen.' 'When the Messiah comes' – which meant never! On the other hand, some pious Jews were more hopeful. There were mock wedding invitations which stated that, 'The marriage celebrations of Abie and Sadie would take place in Jerusalem (Old City) in the presence of King Messiah himself. Nectar and Leviathan would be served on crockery of gold.'

But in small letters at the bottom of the invitation was written 'And if King Messiah has tarried (Habakkuk 2.3) then go instead to Cohen's Kosher Bakery by Whitechapel Station for lemon tea and chopped herring bagels'.

This ambivalence was expressed in our greetings. We couldn't wish each other 'Merry Christmas' – we might forget ourselves and wish it to a rabbi (aller wei – all woe!). But many did and do combine together the greetings of Christmas and Chanukah, the closest Jewish festival which celebrates the triumph of the Maccabees. If you're not Jewish, I wouldn't risk it. It might sound rather saucy. In Britain, the combined greeting is Chatzmus, in Germany it was Weihnukah.

My first substantial religious experience

This took place on or rather soon after my Confirmation – my Bar Mitzvah in Hebrew – and this was the way of it. In 1942 the windows of our London house got blown in and I was again hurriedly blown out into the country, which I detested. Then in 1943, just as hurriedly, I was summoned back to London. In the confusion my parents had forgotten about my Bar Mitzvah so they hired a poor refugee to do a 'rush job' on me. In this rite of passage I had to chant, in a public service, some verses from the synagogue Torah scroll on which was written the five books of Moses, and then – ritually at least – I became a man.

The signs were not auspicious: my refugee teacher said that my Confirmation was a blasphemy, what with me being a self-confessed atheist Marxist who had had no Jewish religious instruction after the war started, and had been singing loud and resounding Christian hymns in school assembly, which I enjoyed; but they didn't count – or counted against me.

And I agreed with him when I discovered that my portion of text concerned the ancient sacrifice of birds – pigeons I think – which I mentally rejected as irrelevant to my life and problems. Nevertheless we soldiered on: he was in need of his pittance, and I was lured by the promise of presents and a party with my Aunt Lil's wartime strudel.

My problems! I was foxed by the whole business of puberty; but I knew better than to ask my parents or any adult about it. They weren't up to it, being even more evasive about it than they were about religion. I intuited, because I knew I was a peculiar boy, that there would be trouble ahead, though I couldn't see the form it would take. (Everybody was dishonest about sex at that time.) And did I even want to become a Jew? I decided it wouldn't make any difference to my chances of survival if I stayed in or opted out. The Nazis, if and when they invaded, wouldn't make any nice distinctions about which Jews were next for the gas chambers, kosher or secular.

The ceremony went off better than I expected. I chanted my sacrifice passage with feeling, and the rabbi, who didn't know me, said some nice things about me, which astounded my parents, and I purred thinking about the presents and apple strudel ahead.

The next day I was sent to give a charity donation to the rabbi. He was at a meeting, and I waited in the women's gallery of the empty silent synagogue, looking down at the dais with its Ark and Scroll where the travesty of my Bar Mitzvah had taken place. Being a pragmatic kid I decided to be generous and give God a chance: I couldn't talk to anyone else about what was worrying me.

So I spoke aloud into the silence the real problems of my life, incidentally telling him that I took a dim view of him and whatever he stood for. I felt like being honest not just to him, if he existed, but also to myself. I wondered if I'd be struck dead by a thunderbolt. Instead something inside me said, 'Bravo – you might not have become a man but at least you've become an adult.' It was odd to find courage to be honest in such a hotbed of avoidance, superstition and bird sacrifice – amid all that 'opium of the masses'.

I puzzled over my Confirmation experience when I took a holiday from Marx. I tried to tell the 'comrades' about what happened in the synagogue. But like the over-certain religious lot, they didn't want to listen. They already knew the truth, so inconvenient honesty wasn't necessary – even dangerous. I decided that the public ceremony meant little to me but the silent part did. I could tell my own truth to myself in it.

So I decided to pop in occasionally to other empty places of worship and see if it happened there too. Instead of going on a pub crawl, I'd go on a synagogue, chapel or church crawl, and see what I trawled up from those murky superstition-infected depths. At that time there were no counsellors or therapists around, and these were the only places I knew where I could be honest. I told enquiring friends that I went into them because they were rich in history and therefore good for my studies. But in truth they were more illuminating about my present, and about the anger, despair and confusion of my puberty and adolescence than about any academic past.

I recommend a similar tour if you're also an intending God-seeker. Be prepared to work through various layers of embarrassment before you get to the bliss, illumination or happy-clappy part. There's an awful lot of fluff in your mind.

Here are examples of what I still encounter which might help you to persevere. Many want to bolt as soon as they get into the God business. Stick it out! The truth might make you free, as the Gospel says, but it doesn't necessarily make you comfortable. That's the cherry on the cake which may come later.

I wouldn't worry about the current attacks on belief. God can be neither proved nor disproved. Just enjoy your transcendental explorations and see where they lead.

Lord Harries (former Bishop of Oxford) said over the radio, 'That there probably is no God has the corollary that there might possibly be one.' But what God is for *you* might take a lifetime or longer to work out.

The prophet Jeremiah says, 'If you seek me with all your heart, I shall let you find me, says the Lord.'

You've started on a game of celestial hide and seek!

God Direct

My dud Confirmation and its surprising sequel in the silent gallery gave a special slant to my religious search, turning it first into a God search, one result of which is this guide for Godseekers.

Are the two searches that different? There is certainly a difference of emphasis according to which starts up first, though each usually leads into the other.

I was thirteen when all this happened, and naturally the needs and demands of my body had taken over in their urgency those of my mind, which were well developed, and those of my soul, whose existence I didn't acknowledge.

Now if you're a 'straight' kid, the world is more or less adjusted to your bodily needs – in my time the back row of the cinema was the recognized place of research, the results of which were compared and collated in the school playground. Twanging brassière straps was the supreme delight.

But being a homo child (later 'gay'), you were on your own. You entered into a world of shadows, furtive pick-ups, blackmail, half lies, whole lies, and even trial and imprisonment. Unfortunately I had no brothers to enlighten me, and sex was a subject I don't think my parents were very good at; it took a long time for them to get their act together. I remember feeling sorry for them while they worried about me, because obviously my withdrawal into myself was not normal.

I tried parent substitutes but got no joy or accurate information from any of them. One rabbi turned me out, another pitied me but said nothing, and the Christian clergymen I got to know weren't straight with me either. They lured me into unburdening myself and, when I did just that, they vanished over the horizon so fast I couldn't see them for dust. They either didn't know that much or, if they did, they weren't telling me. With hindsight, I don't blame them. As I had rejected my body, I must have been a very unattractive specimen – untidy, dirty, unshaven and gauche. I thought I looked like a monster and it was the first triumph of my analyst that he forced me to look into a mirror and do a dispassionate check-list on myself. He was right – I had the normal two legs, the normal proportions, the usual bits – I was just like everybody else.

To my horror the left-wing lot were the same as the church and synagogue lot. Stalin threw gays into gulags, Hitler threw them into concentration camps, and Franco, Mussolini, the Gang of Five and Communist Albania were no better. There was no room at the inn for 'deviants' even in the free-thinking collectives of the Zionists who just replicated the limited mores of good old bourgeois Golders Green on the other side of the Mediterranean, though they didn't realize it.

So I had to venture into the strange country of the rejected alone. And yet not alone! Because in silent places of worship I put God to the test and turned to him.

Well, for one thing he didn't seem surprised or judgemental and, after all – he made me, I didn't make myself. Then he told me to look and listen, which I did, and a wave of compassion came over me – for me and others like me. I nearly drowned in it. He had put me in the company of those who didn't fit in, a Jew among Jews, and it was hell. I made a vow when I entered official religion that no child would have to suffer my experience if I could help it.

Now what I wanted wasn't exotic or revolutionary. I wanted just what all my classmates wanted as a matter of course – the companionship of a 'steady' and, eventually, a home for two rather like my grandparents' home. But as I couldn't rely on society to get me there, I needed a source of courage and strength to get it myself.

To my astonishment, I found both in empty chapels talking to Whomsoever-Whatsoever, Jesus and Fred, and from within me lying on an analyst's couch in King's Cross. You needed a lot of spirituality and honesty for the latter, and I acquired both only gradually. If this surprises you, dear Godseeker, it also surprised me. For this I put up with all the destructive slurs on sexual minorities and their relationships that were common then in ecclesiastical circles and which are still around. I know that a lot of official religions say they love us 'queers'. Well, if they are our friends, who needs enemies?

Fred works in peculiar ways. It was my dad Confirmation and my 'sinful longings' which started me off on my spiritual journey. Because of them, I never confused religion with respectability. Like many gays, I fell in love with Love first, and only later applied it to my relationships.

And what about the Bible? Well, there's not much about the whole business in the Bible; a line or two with a strong caution against dressing up in women's clothes (which didn't apply to me) accompanied by the word 'abomination' for using a man like a woman, and there was some steamy language about David, who seemed to me to be bi-sexual. There was nothing explicitly said about being gay in the Gospels or the Koran for that matter. Poor Old Mother Riley and pantomime dames! By the way, also nothing about lesbian women. In such a macho society, I suppose what women did among themselves was not taken seriously. Bronze Age Middle Eastern society was very macho, with lots of concubines and a high infant mortality rate; the name of the game was survival. Very different from our own overpopulated planet.

As for 'abomination': if, dear Godseeker, this term worries you, I suggest you do some simple research: consult reference books and look up all the issues which were labelled that way. They are a motley lot, many of which are now irrelevant or fallen by the wayside or absorbed by common sense.

This has been a long detour, but it was necessary to explain why spirituality was not a fringe fashion for me but a very necessary help to deal with the urgent problem of puberty and its testosterone, which I was just beginning to face. It was such powerful stuff, religion wouldn't do; I needed God Direct.

'Away from here'

The Second World War had just ended; I was fifteen and felt the call to travel. Where to I didn't know, just 'away from here'. I was looking for something but I didn't know what.

I packed a surplus army rucksack and, bent double by its weight, joined the line of adolescent Rumpelstiltskins lining the roads to the Continent, hiking and hitchhiking wherever – like the early Celtic saints who put out to sea in their coracles making for wherever the winds and tides of God bore them.

On the crossroads outside Calais I started hitching. If my first lift was going north, I would go north, and the holiday would be Amsterdam and more Amsterdam. If it went south it was the Med, monasteries and Venice.

On the straight dusty roads of France I joined up with an American girl who carried a pepper pot as a weapon to defend her honour. She sussed out early on that I was no threat, as she was the wrong sex for me and I was the wrong sex full stop. (It was she who began to enlighten me about my situation – the rabbis, clerics and youth leaders were too scared.) She waggled her thumb and lifted a leg by the side of the road and, when a car stopped, I burst out from behind the bush where I was lurking. The drivers usually wanted just her and I didn't blame them, as I looked unkempt and fearsome, with an excited wild look. I was honest enough to admit that I wouldn't have stopped for myself. She eventually decided that I was an impediment to her progress, which was true, and left me abruptly, leaving me meticulously fairly with half our communal baguette and a whole tomato.

Almost crazy with loneliness, a dot in that flat dusty landscape with its straight endless roads, I eventually stumbled over one of the new worker priests in a hedge. He taught me how to serve Mass for him in the hedgerow, and one morning told me I could take Communion, which I appreciated. It was the same as the Friday evening Sabbath sanctification of bread and wine in my dead granny's home. Communion, he said, was not a reward for good behaviour but a help to find my bearings. It made me feel good but I didn't understand the fuss made about it. It was he who told me to ditch my road map. What I was looking for was not another town or Roman ruin but my eternal home. He was my first real religious teacher. He showed me the way ahead, my next step. 'Seek and ye shall find! If you are really looking for teachers you don't just find them, they happen,' he had said to me.

Not long after my hedgerow priest went his own way I arrived at a youth hostel where they had no room at the inn. It was jam packed with youngsters and oldsters making their way to Provence on pennies, to the gold coast of Nice, Cannes and St Raphael. I was locked out with a young German. We were allowed to sleep on the veranda. I had a sleeping-bag, he had a blanket, and we snuggled together against the cold. He shared his cigarette with me – two orphans in the storm. We talked. His father had died on the eastern front and his mother had married again. He had been one of the last Hitler Youth in his town and was making his way to South America, not being able to bear the shame of Germany's defeat.

I told him I was a Jew defeated by life, sex and loneliness. Before he left for Marseilles in the morning, we embraced and he said he would never hurt Jews again. 'Promises, promises!' But perhaps he meant it because he left me one of his last cigarettes. And I said a clumsy prayer for him as the priest had taught me.

In a short time I had learnt lessons in holiness and stretched my compassion far beyond the normal. The road I was now travelling was different from the one I had started out on; I hadn't had enough sex to know whether I was a man but, my Marxist materialism notwithstanding, I began to wonder if I had a soul.

Dear Godseeker, I have told you this adolescent episode not just as sentimental reminiscence but to emphasize an important lesson. To make a spiritual journey inside you, you may also have to make a physical journey outside you. I began to understand the call to my ancestor Abraham, 'Get thee out of thy country . . . and to a land which thou knowest not of.'

In your own home, your possessions and your social obligations defend you against the unexpected, the surprise of God, or Heaven, or whatever you may call that other soul dimension.

Now it is not necessary to hitch-hike through recently liberated France to free yourself. It can happen at a business cocktail party. While jabbering social nothings thirteen to the dozen, a part of you separates from you (as it were) and, from somewhere near the ceiling, looks down with detachment and compassion. Sometimes you watch your whole life. It is not an uncommon experience. To view one's life like that, many go to a retreat house or make a pilgrimage. If the spiritual energy is too foreign and alarming, be careful about secularizing it. It might express itself in a one-night stand, swift sex or drink. They are ways of avoidance. Love of God and love of sex are very closely related. I understand the hesitation very well. I experience it myself before going on a retreat.

Here are some guide books for your journey – my personal selection. Many people have trodden the road into this other dimension before you and left books of their experience and the terrain to be traversed.

The Dharma Bums by Jack Kerouac – very much 'of its time', which was my time, the 1960s.

Pilgrim's Progress by John Bunyan – a wonderfully accurate summary of the world for Godseekers and spiritual hitch-hikers. There's Giant Despair with his dreadful wife at Doubting Castle within you and outside you in real life. In the modern flesh and blood of the rat-race society, all the characters of Vanity Fair. As I get older, the different ways people cross the River of Death are becoming increasingly relevant; but that is for later. The celestial city, like all human attempts at credible heavens and hells, doesn't seem as real as the journey to it.

Try *The Book of Margery Kempe*, the medieval patroness of packaged holidays (my award). She was born in 1364, had about fourteen children, and went on pilgrimages to Rome, Jerusalem, Santiago, North Germany, etc., etc. She met Julian of Norwich, and one wonders how the two mystic autobiographical ladies got on. Julian, who never had children, talks of the Motherhood of God, while Margery never mentions her many children at all. What I like about her is that, as well as seeking the higher truth, she is honest on the lower slopes; a rare virtue in religion.

After she was converted, she made a carnal assignation with a man behind a holy statue in King's Lynn church. But when he met her, he told her she was just ordure and he only wanted to test her. What a brute! But how courageous of her to admit to being stood up! Most saints admit to sins before their conversion but not after, and never such humiliating ones. Poor Margery! She was proposed to by God the Father in a mystic marriage, but she was reluctant. She didn't want an old man but young Jesus who sat at the bottom of her bed in a purple robe. I would have felt the same. Of course, in the end, being a pious woman, she accepted God the Father and, at their nuptials, anybody who was somebody in heaven was invited.

On a more worldly level, she could be more than kind and very, very courageous. 'I've heard that you are a very naughty woman,' the powerful Archbishop of York said to her. 'And I have heard that you are a very naughty Archbishop,' she replied. How she got away with it I do not know. I think many people, like you or me, would have found her impossible – but an innocent with a good heart. A second- or third-class saint – but all the better for that!

Another truth I learned from my journey of enlightenment came to me in the departure lounge of my very first flight. I didn't know how to phrase it then; but I do now. I realized that my real home was not in this world at all but in another dimension, and it was called heaven. This was a mind-boggling discovery, and the evidence is that nearly all the books I have written have got Heaven in their title.

'Heav'n, heav'n, I'm gonna sing all over God's heav'n!'

I could not have learned those truths in lower-middle-class London suburbia.

And then . . .

. . . the seeds of eternity You have planted among us . . .
(The Jewish liturgy)

My parents were united in wanting to get me and them out of the poverty of London's East End by becoming a professional with a house in Highgate or Hampstead. But I told them I wanted to become a revolutionary and blow up the world because I was finding adolescence too difficult and knew I was heading for a breakdown.

After dramatics from all sides it was agreed that, provided I got a degree, I could go to hell whichever way I pleased. My mother cried – the end of her illusion! I placated her, in part, by promising not to wear a beard and by getting a degree first.

So I sat in the local library and applied to every university and college listed, including some women's colleges (though I didn't know it) who replied to a Miss Blue, puzzled not by her politics but by her gender. With relief I accepted a place at all-male Balliol College, Oxford, which, it was rumoured, welcomed Scots, Blacks and Jews.

Sixty years ago I was an early arriver. I sat in Balliol College Library in Oxford, moodily turning the pages of my very first set book, the Venerable Bede's *Ecclesiastical History of the English People.* What was a Venerable? And why Ecclesiastical? And in medieval Latin! It didn't fit a scientific revolutionary like me. As adolescents do, I blamed the mess on my parents. But being honest, I realized their responsibility had ended. I was beginning to know what hell was like. I was in it!

Impatiently I leafed through Bede's pages – and read about tough butch Anglian kings giving their finest horses to Celtic hermits who owned nothing, who then gave them on to peasants with less than nothing.

I was touched and startled. I'd fallen through a time-warp and landed in the world of my pious, almost illiterate Yiddish granny, who extended her soup to feed the destitute, and my ma, who'd given away her winter coat – almost forgotten memories of my early childhood.

Goodness has a golden aura; whether in Bede's England or Petticoat Lane. The seeds they planted of another world with other values began to glow in me. I had tried to go to hell but was getting pulled in another direction.

This startled me. It wasn't what I had expected. Now I'd always accepted, irrationally for a Marxist, that Jews had a holy history;

with the Bible you couldn't miss it. But this country, England, my country, had its own holy history too. So I was also the inheritor of Bede, Bunyan, and Blake's Jerusalem 'in England's green and pleasant land'. I needed to bring the two together in me – a task that awaits all who settle here in peace.

I then learned another unscheduled lesson in manners which, in England, often substitutes for morals, at a Balliol dance. Many girls wore the then fashionable boned strapless dresses. One girl twirled but her top didn't. Her partner covered her and led her away. 'Poor girl,' I said to my own partner. 'How embarrassing.' 'I don't know what you're talking about,' she said. 'A lady only sees what she's supposed to see and a gentleman likewise.'

At Oxford I fell in love with this country – not just its piety but its mysticism and those mysterious manners. To my parents' surprise, I returned an almost Anglican gentleman. They thought I was taking the mickey – perhaps I was, but only a bit.

It was then I began to experience a feeling that was strange to me. I felt as if I was being attracted to an unknown world which I had forgotten since early childhood – a world not outside me but inside me. I remembered one of those curious rabbi's tales, 'What is the origin of that cleft on your forehead between your two eyes?' a rabbi asked and, getting no reply, supplied the answer himself – as rabbis are wont to do. 'Before you are born an angel tells you all the important things that will happen to you in life and about where you come from and where you will go; the dimension from which you came and to which you will return. An angel then knocks you with a hammer between the eyes, which accounts for the cleft, and you forget it all. But occasionally in life, when you stumble on something really important, you feel you are remembering what you already possess – not learning it afresh.'

I have spoken to other Godseekers: many of them share this experience of mine, which is that heaven, or the spiritual world, is already known to us from long ago, and that some attraction or force pulls us towards it and, even if we decide to go to hell, our true destination is heaven.

I puzzled over these experiences in college chapels – of which Oxford has a super-abundance. Some were drear and some smart and shiny. But it was in Balliol library that a seed flowered in me.

Dear Godseeker, return to your early childhood and to your burgeoning soul.

An East European footnote

My East European granny brought me up on the prejudices of her homeland, and her frightful stories still rattle round my mind. A Christian girl is found drowned near a Jewish village. 'Flee!' shouts the rabbi, 'before a pogrom starts.' Terrified people panic when a man bursts in. 'Thank God,' he shouts tearfully, 'we're saved. The drowned girl was Jewish.'

It's better Granny's dead because, in the expanded European Union, she'd be back with the homeland she fled from.

But all Europe is worm eaten with prejudice, including us. Northern Ireland explodes with it. A girl remarked, 'On the border they don't give us lifts because we're Welsh.' Scottish students told me they resented being stereotyped by the English as mean, and that calling Queen Elizabeth the Second, not the First, insulted Scottish history. I told them about a performance in Edinburgh where continental tourists and Irish were welcomed but visitors from south of the border were told they were only wanted for their money.

If there's a real economic crash and all the worms of prejudice crawl out, new Europe could blow apart like old Yugoslavia, which had a common currency and constitution for 50 years before it disintegrated in murder. Tax adjustments aren't enough. We've got to exorcise old ghosts.

But to exorcise them we must understand them. In our crowded continent we're prejudiced against people who seem to stand in our way or deny us something we think is ours. So people with chips on their shoulders are open to prejudice and people secure in themselves are resistant. To prevent prejudice taking over, check out its truth, and who is manipulating it. Also be big enough to accept blame because what you hate in others is what you can't stand in yourself. Get to know personally the people you're prejudiced against.

I'll do my bit and visit granny's homeland, which I've always avoided. The dead must bury their dead before new life begins. 'Hath not one father created us? Are we not brethren?'

Whatever Europe becomes, a free trade association or a union, it will require inner work from each of us. Some youngsters say 'Together we'll become skilled lovers like the French overnight, patient like us British, disciplined as Germans and joyous as Italians.' Ah, but if we don't exorcise our prejudices we could become louts in London, with the patience of Parisians, the discipline of Italians, and the gaiety of Germans. And granny's ghost would scream, 'I told you so!'

You need a lot of God to exorcise so many ghosts!

Chapter 3

Falling in Love and its Results

Introduction

One Thursday morning in November 1950, I fell in love with Love – just like popular songs say.

The world remained the same – no miracles happened, just the occasional surprise or wonder or coincidence. But I did see the world in a different way, with different lights and shadows. And, at the same time, the echo of that voice in me became a friend, a guide whom I could talk to. I couldn't work out whether it was faith or testosterone. But beggars can't be choosers, so I went along with it.

This all started up in a Quaker Meeting House in St Giles in Oxford. The rest of my life has been spent working out what truly happened. Many Godseekers like you and me experience a defining moment like that.

About the same time, or shortly after, I fell by accident into analysis by Leslie Shepard, a pupil of Wilhelm Reich, Freud's most radical pupil. Looking back, I am very grateful to him, to God, to Reich and to the Quakers. They fitted together beautifully because you can't know much more about God than you know about yourself.

Both events refashioned me. It was like a new birth, chill but hopeful. Somewhat fearfully, I began to face the future. It was more complex than I thought.

I fall among Quakers

I have told this story in other places but I repeat it here because it was the decisive experience that turned me round from a living death in a psychiatric ward after a badly judged semi-suicide attempt – in retrospect a clumsy cry for help at university by a student suffering from adolescence, pimples, loneliness, and too much testosterone. You often have to hit bottom before any turn-around can happen, and it happened to me at a Quaker Meeting, the first I'd ever attended.

Many Godseekers have this 'resurrection' experience because, when you do touch bottom, you really pray instead of toying with prayer. It's when you're drowning that you shout 'Help!' and, to your surprise, help comes because, however humble and basic, that's the sincere prayer, the prayer of your heart.

Religion had changed and was no longer polite or bitchy arguments about rites and rituals, or irrelevant arguments about what came before the Big Bang – if there was a 'before' or a 'Big Bang' - or who has the freehold of the Wailing Wall. My new religion was about real resurrection, which had become my daily bread, not debating society cake.

Never despise your problems – I think all Godseekers know from their own life experience that problems may be minuses in this worldly life but plusses in that dimension described as the life of the world to come or the life of the soul. As a rabbi teacher once said to me, 'Only your problems and failures will teach you charity and humility and what it's like to be at the wrong end of the stick.' I think of this every time I pass by the derelicts outside London stations or hovering outside the doors of supermarkets.

Thinking back to those times, there was a build-up to my experience; it didn't just come out of the blue or happen as suddenly as I pretended to other people and to myself. Simone Weil says that to find the true God may not be possible at first, but what we can do is prepare the ground by eliminating our false gods. My false god at that time, the late 1940s and early 1950s, was Stalinism, a very unoriginal choice, but understandable, because if Stalin had not entered the war, albeit unwillingly, I and many others like me would have gone up in a puff of smoke from the gas chambers.

My false god broke in pieces when I was marching in a Stalinist procession shouting out the names of his East European mafia. Suddenly I said to myself, 'This is idolatry – not rationality.' I left the procession and took refuge in an indo-pak restaurant, gobbling hot curry while brooding over how I'd been taken for a ride. I never rejoined the procession. But this left an awful hole in my life. How could I sublimate my sexual urges now?

This very personal problem became even more pressing after I took tea with my girlfriend at another Oxford college. We were a marriage of two minds but not so together in other parts of our anatomy. I only knew that when we got to 'necking' there was no erotic response in me. What I wanted sexually was then as criminal in capitalist London as it was in socialist Moscow. I gave up. I couldn't cope and dolefully made my way from her college to mine. The skies were grey outside and my thoughts were even greyer inside. Life had dealt me a hand I couldn't play. The rain started to pour down and I took refuge in a doorway in St Giles. The skies were weeping and I was crying too – great tears of self-pity.

The door opened unexpectedly – a lady (Miss Joachim, I learned later) took me by the hand and beckoned me into a quiet Quaker Meeting for farmers, who testified soberly and pleasantly. They came on Thursdays because they had nobody on Sundays to look after their animals. Their kindness and purity got to me and touched me. At first I said to myself, 'What is a yiddisher boy like me doing in a place like this?' And then I wondered if they were all nutty – speaking to some being who wasn't there. But you catch religion as you catch measles: without willing it. And then I stepped inside and testified in plangent Jewish style from the depths of my tormented Semitic East European Slavic being. They didn't sit up, and I didn't care if they did or not because I was beyond exhibitionism. I wasn't putting anything on. I was in a Dostoyevskian nightmare, known to many in a severe depression, which is often a diving-board into the divine for Godseekers. I just asked a deity in whom I didn't believe to make some sense of my misery. The Quaker farmers must have thought this great stuff, because the chairman of the meeting shook my hand when it ended. I received an English understated but approving accolade, and Miss Joachim asked me to tea.

But what was more important, a message did get through to me from outside me – from that dimension beyond the cosmos – or which welled up from deep inside me; the first explanation felt more right. The message was muddling, yet clear. I should turn my miseries upside down, invert them and then look at them in another light. In the light of that dimension, the facts hadn't changed but their meaning had.

'Faites vos jeux!' ('Place your bets!'): I decided to take a calculated leap and, for a while at least, to bet on God and see what happened. Tentatively I thanked a God I didn't believe in for all my problems. Without them I would be a self-satisfied prig or a sharp suburban businessman. With them I could learn mercy and self-honesty and what it was like to be at the other end of the stick. There was no other way I would ever feel such wisdom. My problems might be a grace of God if he existed rather than his punishment. This made me feel very chosen and very important. One of the nice things about Christianity was that it made much of an individual and not just a collective. It was a private one-to-one relationship between me and Whatever. A shift also took place inside of me. I went into overdrive and got ecstatic about the pleasure of giving, so, after the service, I started giving away things. The God thing or Jesus thing had got to me, I decided, and had turned me upside down, inside out, and topsy-turvy. What I was experiencing was a rebirth of my soul, which I had lost or dismissed in London's East End at the age of five. I was no longer a mere mind – I could now proceed from a feeling centre. It was a bit atrophied, but new life was getting pumped into it.

My college room-mate, Robin, approved when I told him about it, though he was rightly apprehensive about the wild dispersal of my possessions (and some of his, too) to whoever asked, and surprised fellow students who didn't even ask – it wasn't just topsy-turvy – it was over the top.

But I left that meeting light and soufflé-ish giving away my velvet tie to a surprised acquaintance, and not knowing what had hit me.

My revelation came not in a church but in a cake shop. I was queuing up for my piece of Fuller's walnut cake, idly listening to the background radio. The words of the song actually were 'Falling in love with love is only make believe' but I heard it as 'Falling in love with love *isn't* just make believe', which is what I felt. I had fallen in love with Love and it was re-programming me. If you think love is Christianity, well maybe I was a Christian in part! If you think Christianity is belief in creeds and surplices and institutions, then I wasn't.

This came out very clearly when Christian friends decided I should read the New Testament and be baptized. Well, I never fell into the font: the New Testament was too elitist ('many are called and few are chosen') and extremist ('if your eye offends you, pluck it out'). There was more anger in it than I expected, a fair amount of anti-Judaism, and stories more mystic than real. If I'd been born into it I would have stuck to it – but I wasn't. So I wavered and didn't.

But what I did get was that I could fall in love with Love, as I've said, that love could have a human face, and the kernel of it all was generosity. It also needed honest foundations.

Something else happened at that Quaker Meeting. I started to speak to an imaginary voice, which was no big deal as I'd inhabited a fantasy world for years. But there was a difference: in this new fantasy world the Voice spoke back, and its/his/her answers weren't the ones I expected. 'Do I become Christian?' I asked him. He was disinterested. 'That's your business,' he said. But if I got mean or lied to myself, he got quite stroppy.

I have never forgotten this experience. At retreats, while others have brooded over scriptural texts, I have brooded over what this voice/this presence was telling me.

It told me that I was not a believer but a pragmatic truster. I had gone into religion because I had problems, and I stayed with it because it worked. I myself was the evidence for what I trusted. I'd learned that, if you face problems, they turn inside out. So I tried not to pray for problems to disappear, but for courage to face them. I wasn't quite sure if I was in love, but I had found a True Friend in High Places; which was more than I'd had before and more than I ever expected. I enjoyed sitting next to him without speaking. I wasn't schizoid, and I wasn't a ventriloquist.

My call

I finally KO'd my poor parents by ringing them from Oxford to bring the glad tidings – that I wanted to become a monk or a Quaker.

There was a silence at the other end and the line crackled with my ma's displeasure. 'Lionel,' she said, 'you're doing this to spite us – after all the hard work your father and I have done to get you up there. You should be ashamed of yourself. So help me, I'll commit suicide.' 'And your father too,' she added for good measure.

I was indignant. I wasn't doing it to spite them at all, at least not much. I'd caught religion like measles, enjoyed it and suddenly decided that this was for me. It's been the unlikeliest but best decision I've ever taken.

Dear Godseeker, here are some unofficial tips if the call comes to you too. It can come to anybody, so why not you? You'll need determination because everybody tries to put you off. You're not even sure yourself. After all, your life hasn't been that ministerial. Well, neither was mine! Your self-doubt will at least stop you getting too grand for your own good. And this is important because you have to learn humility, which doesn't mean hours of knee work or passing diplomas in it.

I learned some humility from the stories and jokes they told me in old-age homes. The local minister makes his parochial call and to his irritation there is no red carpet awaiting him. And when he marches in, the matron isn't even there to greet him. Irritably he grabs an old man tottering to the loo on his zimmer frame. 'Don't you know who I am?' he announces. The oldie looks at him kindly. 'Don't worry,' he says, 'it happens to lots of us. Go over to nurse there. She'll tell you!'

If you decide (or rather your voice tells you) to become a minister as well, you'll certainly need humility to cope with the put-downs all ministers get. An old man snores during your sermon. You shake him awake. 'You didn't listen to a word I said,' you tell him. 'That just shows how much I trust you, Rabbi!' he answers.

Here is some unofficial advice. If you can laugh at yourself, you'll do very well, not just in the ministry, but in life. Smiles debunk false pride, which is a great temptation when you prance around in robes and vestments, smoothing their silk or pure wool!

Advice to fellow Godseekers after a 'big' experience

I'd go along with it, but remember you might have a rocky ride integrating it with the rest of your life. Prepare to be inconsistent for a while.

Don't expect everybody around you to greet the change with the same enthusiasm as you. Once again I rang my mother from Oxford – this time to tell her that I had a call to the Rabbinate. There was silence at the other end and I thought rather smugly that my mother was speechless with joy at my return to the fold. Not a bit. When she recovered speech, she said once again, 'Lionel you're doing it to spite us. All our lives your father and I have worked our fingers to the bone to get you out of the ghetto, and what do you do when you get to Oxford, you jump right back into it again.' 'You should be ashamed of yourself. You've done it to spite us,' she repeated and slammed down the phone. In the end she became accustomed to the idea, especially after I told her rabbis can't become Anglo-Catholic priests ('I'll commit suicide and your father too') or Hindu swamis with begging-bowls outside Golders Green Station where her friends and foes passed by.

Ponder what actually happened! Don't rush to conclusions!

In any messages to you there'll be a bit of Whomsoever-Whatsoever and a lot of your own manipulative neurotics. Most visionaries and hearers of voices are a bit that way inclined. If you're a student, are you using all this to avoid an exam you haven't done the work for? I did! Even if that's true, it doesn't invalidate your experience or your 'call'.

If your experience makes you kinder, more generous and more honest to yourself about yourself, then you're on pretty solid ground (the last of the three is the most difficult). Go for it!

If it makes you manipulative, judgemental and puffed up, forget it and try again later.

Chapter 4

Repeated Later – The Positive Consequences of Religious Experience

In a chapel

Dear Godseeker,

Previously God found you – now it's your turn to find him/her/it. His relationship to his creatures may be enigmatic, but usually if you don't ask, you don't get – 'Ask and ye shall receive.'

Make yourself comfy in a chapel or place of worship, but not during a service. Other people can be around if they're on the same track as you: in fact, their presence is helpful because they reassure you that you're not going nuts talking to someone who isn't there.

Your first temptation is to jazz it up. Don't worry about it – the 'religious' froth and razzmatazz will drop away as you get more convinced about what you're doing and of its validity and reality in your day-to-day life. How do Godseekers jazz it up? Well, if you half shut your eyes you can see mistily/mystically through your lashes or bi-focals and in retrospect this can become a vision. In the Middle Ages people saw angels that way, as do little children today. That's the way angels become visible round the Sabbath table, the spirit of Elijah at Passover time, Father Christmas and Rudolph the Red-Nosed Reindeer. Visions of the saints, Jesus and wonder rabbis respond to the same treatment.

Why do we do this? Because we don't have enough confidence in the reality of the spiritual world. We want to have it buttressed and made more solid by confirmation in the material world. Don't be embarrassed – it's a feature of a lot of early (and later) religious literature, and occurs frequently in the Old and New Testaments. But the real evidence of the spiritual world is spiritual, just as the reward for doing a good deed is another good deed.

Sometimes an inner voice speaks in you straight away, or a moment of enlightenment happens just like that. But usually you have to do a lot of digging. You're Salome and there are a lot of veils you have to divest. It's rather like separating the layers of an onion. The first layer/veil is that of embarrassment. Speaking to a being who isn't there – and you a grown adult too! The presence of other grown adults around doing the same thing should reassure you. When you've got beyond that, irrelevant worries crowd in. Some people think that the Devil is trying to de-rail them. It can certainly feel like that, and I've experienced it too, though I'm too much a monotheist and a paid-up Freudian to permit myself to take devil images uncritically. Your devils are often the unloved or unacknowledged bits of you.

I'd put it this way: there's a part of you which feels uncomfortable with the spiritual or divine. You might be afraid you've stirred up more than you bargained for, and you're right – you have. It's spooky and you'll want to run back to the solid and familiar. Resist! Go on with what you're doing – otherwise you'll despise yourself.

After this comes a wave of feelings and recollections more usual on a psychoanalyst's couch. And why not? Life is hard, and you're probably Godseeking because you've got problems. Let it all hang out! You might be frightened of the truth, but God isn't.

Crying is permitted, but don't sob, because it's too noisy and distracting for the other Godseekers present.

After the tears and the debris of your life and past feelings fade out or get washed away, there often comes a moment of quietness.

You cease to try so hard, you don't try at all. An inner peace wells up in you without you trying anything. You accept the life around you. Some people begin to giggle over their problems. Many of them are only as important or foolish as you make them. You feel like Julian of Norwich and say to yourself, 'All will be well, and all will be well and all will be very well.'

There is no need to do anything: just enjoy sitting and then pack up your belongings and, at a nearby café, treat yourself to coffee and a custard cake or a muffin. Somewhere on the way back home you will find yourself impelled to do a good deed. The opportunities are everywhere if you are not tied up in knots of ego. A bit of translation from inner experience into worldly life is a good thing. It fixes your experience in your memory and you begin to trust it. All good deeds leave a glow behind them. It is a momentary foretaste of heaven in this world.

You can get addicted to such moments: your love affair has started.

Sometimes – many times – you don't realize fully what's happened to you or what's being said in you until much later. A silly silence in a chapel leaves only a pretty banal thought or word which just keeps surfacing, and you finally realize that there was a meeting; though it didn't work as you expected.

Life's a jest

> *Life's a jest and all things show it*
> *I thought so once and now I know it.*
> John Gay's epitaph (author of *The Beggar's Opera*)

An odd effect of the God experience was that it changed my life and outlook in a very unexpected way and, over half a century later, I am still reeling and surprised by the effects of it. It wasn't what I expected at all.

Marxism had made me an earnest and grim young man, a junior version of old boy Marx himself, tortured by piles as he brooded over the coming collapse which actually happened, though not in the way he expected. I gloomily intended to sacrifice myself for my fellow men, though actually I didn't like them very much, but I took comfort in the fact that after the bloody revolution they would all be changed into muscular clear-eyed heroes and heroines, going forward with me to meet the chilly new dawn.

The future was described in our marching song 'Soviet Land': 'Where youth has always hope and old age is always respected'. It was all very puritan and cheerless. And they were worse about gay sex than the debauched capitalists. And the collective Zionist ideal was also pretty grim. In the shadow of the Holocaust, I would become a silent peasant (I even disliked gardening!) and I would spend my life draining a marsh and watering a desert, or vice-versa. It was all too heavy, and it was no wonder I had half a depressive breakdown.

No, the strange thing was that religion made me light and frolicsome. Someone complimented me at Oxford on my one tie (American red roses on a sateen whorls background). I promptly took it off and handed it to him. I discovered that giving was a greater joy than receiving – which I had never realized before. I began to see why the combination of giving and laughter, joined together in the Chassidic rabbis and in St Francis of Assisi, was so appealing. At first I had been oppressed by the tortures of saints and crucifixions that filled the churches I patronized, but even this did not detract from my delirious new love affair with Love. It was my first love affair, and I have never outgrown it.

I began to understand why religion and the love of God have produced so much art and poetry. I began to paint and write the stuff myself – appallingly egotistic but alive, which atheism and agnosticism were not. I began to trust a little, to like the people around me (which is harder than loving them), and to blossom – watered by a little romantic love. I even began to develop a sense of humour, which I had never had before. I could use it on myself and eventually even on my inflated creaky religion.

Of course, in the beginning I was very 'pi' and could only pity outsiders who did not experience the consolations of faith. But I found my personal religion self-correcting. I sat back, forced to realize that it does take two to tango – in prayer as well as on a dance floor. Something beyond me, outside me, was taking a hand in something more important than my education – my re-formation if you like.

As a child I had been very old, and now religion, instead of making me world-weary as I had expected, was making me young again. To my surprise I also became less judgemental about myself as well as other people; I was kinder and less heavy than before.

This, I think, is why religion didn't go the same way as all the other ideologies I had espoused and then given up. I was grateful to Marx and Freud for the truth they had given me which stopped me making a fool of myself in the field of spirituality. I was convinced enough of another presence not to armour myself against truth and common sense. To my Reichian analyst's astonishment, I got through the intense and painful sessions with him only by praying to God for the strength to endure them – and getting it – and then enjoying them and the release they brought. Two other people started analysis at the same time as I did: one committed suicide, and the other got stuck on a negative transference and couldn't continue. I wonder what Wilhelm Reich would have made of that.

I also ceased to be alone. And that doesn't only mean invitations to enjoyable Anglo-Catholic coffee mornings where I was made much of, but the presence of a Presence very much like the 'Guest' in George Herbert's poem.

Now I've reached 80, I know I shall have to go on some retreats to get closer to that Presence once again. I need some help, since my teachers, Fr Gordian Marshall, Rabbi Albert Friedlander, Jannie (Joanna Mary) Hughes, Leslie Shepard and Sr Mary Kelly have died, and I must take the first step towards my next teacher, whoever she or he is.

Remembering nice things

Sometimes there's so much to worry about in the news that I decide to forget sad things for a while and instead remember nice things which aren't newsworthy because they aren't sensational or horrific.

The special one which comes to my mind is an overdue thank-you to the synagogue rooms, meditation rooms, prayer rooms, chapels and churches left open despite the rising cost of insurance and the strictures of ecclesiastical accountants. They provide a user-friendly atmosphere in which people like me who are not conventional believers can meditate and bring together the many varied truths and questions which are coming to us from so many directions, and also where we can ask God or the Divine or Whomso-ever-Whatsoever to be present to us at business meetings and offices, pubs and parties, on boards or in bed, and stick around with us during the coming day.

I started to drop into ruined synagogues, churches and little chapels of remembrance when I went hitch-hiking across Europe after the end of the Second World War. I had hardly any money when I stumbled across some forlorn Capuchin Friars sent back from Abyssinia in a hurry who were as disorientated as I was, rattling around in a vast ruinous monastery. They fed me, for I had developed a mild fever, and never asked me to attend their services or made any windows into my soul. They never wanted any *quid pro quo*, not even a spiritual one, which made me admire them. Instead I just sat silently in their chapel thinking about them and their generosity. Not having any money, I did try to pay them back by teaching them English from the only two books in my rucksack – a James Joyce *Reader* and Bunyan's *Pilgrim's Progress* – with hilarious results.

Later on I also thanked the Sisters in the Tyburn Church near Marble Arch in London who were the only ones who welcomed my dog with me. At that time my office was nearby but I couldn't take my dog into the synagogue when I was meditating and I couldn't leave her alone because she was old, moth-eaten and past it. I found out, through the nuns' confessor, that they had indeed noticed her presence and sent a message to me that they liked her – she seemed such a pious animal. I am not sure if her reputation for piety was deserved. She certainly sat down when everyone else sat down and stood up when they stood up. But I think she was really a conformist at heart with an eye to possible dog chocs for good behaviour. (But that may be the same for most of us!)

I asked the writer, Honor Tracy, in her nursing home about a man in Ireland who said he was a Horse Protestant. He would attend any church where he could tie up his horse in the porch out of the rain. I suppose I was his English counterpart, a Canine Jewish Capuchin. Once again generosity overcame precautions.

I learned a lot from other people praying and meditating in the church. They were such a mixed lot – cleaners from the Mayfair hotels going home after a night's work, the patrons and clientele of West End night clubs, tourists who were starting out early to 'do' London before their afternoon plane took off from Heathrow, some millionaires perhaps, and some beggars certainly. In Judaism religion and family are very close. Here I felt the family of God all around me, though we were all approaching Divinity in different ways and from different directions.

To my surprise and joy, I had found myself a family. My sisters were the Sisters of Sion and my brothers were Dominican and Carmelite Friars and other assorted contemplatives.

Cheering up God

Jewish restaurant joke:
Diner: 'Waiter, the food in this eatery tastes funny.'
Waiter: 'If it tastes so funny, laugh, laugh! Ha ha ha ha ha!'

God is a mystery. Our human race will be dead before we ever know who God is, or what God is, or what his, her or its attributes are, if any. Infinity is beyond our comprehension.

But his extraordinary gift of laughter supports us in this darkness. We are the first animals on the evolutionary ladder to enjoy this grace. Other animals can play but we can joke and even laugh about the pain of living.

A man topples over a cliff into an abyss. As he hurtles down, he saves himself by clutching a small tree growing out of the cliff side. As he dangles in the darkness he prays to God as he has never prayed before. 'If there is a God up there, stretch out your helping hand from heaven and save me!' he shrieks.

To his astonishment a voice thunders from heaven. 'Do not worry,' it says, 'I will put my hand beneath thee to support thee. Just let go and trust in me!' The poor man ponders this in silence and then prays again. 'Is there anyone else up there?' he whispers.

What would you do? That's life!

And here is religious tragedy: 'What makes God happy?' asks a rabbi. 'To see a starving beggar find a ten-pound note in the gutter and then give it into Lost Property.'

And how do I know that jokes give God pleasure? Because he told me so, over 35 years ago when I was asked to give a God-slot on the radio. I asked an old rabbi what I should say. 'Lionel, tell them about the Jewish problem,' he said. But how could I add another problem to their cornflakes when they were already facing the problems of redundancy, strikes and cold. So on the Underground I prayed and the voice of the Lord came unto me saying, 'Lionel, tell them a joke so that they aren't poisoned by their own bitterness. Perform a humble miracle in my name and turn their anger into laughter.'

Which I did, for I remembered this story told me by Rabbi Gryn (may his memory be for a blessing!) about a man for whom everything went wrong: his wife left him, his business went bankrupt and his children walked the streets. As he moodily makes his breakfast, even his toast falls to the floor. But as he picks it up, he cries out in astonishment, 'My God, that toast fell buttered side up. Is it a sign from heaven that my luck has changed?' He wraps up the toast reverently and rushes round to his rabbi. 'You know, rabbi, how bad things have been for me, but look at this toast. It fell buttered side up. Is it a sign that my luck has changed?'

'I must research it with other rabbis and with ecumenical clergy,' said the rabbi excitedly. 'Come back in a week's time and I'll tell you!' The man returned and waited trembling for the rabbi's verdict. 'I'm so, so sorry,' said the rabbi, 'but it's all a terrible mistake: you buttered the wrong side, that's all.'

Now the situation was sad and the joke even sadder, but I heard from many depressed people that my tragic joke had made them giggle so much that they got out of bed and didn't dive back under their duvets again.

So I learned that jokes help you face problems you can't solve, and that turned me from a theologian into an entertainer, which must have made God really laugh because, until then, I had been a toffee-nosed ideologue and cleric. I also learned how black humour had kept religion sane during the Holocaust.

Lastly I realized in prayer that God in his uniqueness might be lonely too. So sometimes at night I tell him not prayers, of which he's probably heard too many, but jokes to ease his suffering over his own creation. Jokes aren't just joking matters.

Humour – on the air!

Dear Godseeker,

The last year wasn't easy but we've survived, and I try to comfort myself sitting on the floor assessing my Chanukah and Christmas loot, handy hankies, real wool socks but wrong size, and a smelly cheese to consume before my household bins it.

I compare present presents to past ones. The best weren't things but the gifts of love and laughter which turned my life around and came after a God experience. Marxism had made me a grim young-ster as I've said – I would sacrifice myself for the toiling masses whom I didn't like much, but then I didn't like anybody much.

But these divine gifts began to lighten me like a soufflé. In empty chapels a power of kindness befriended me. And because it liked me I began to like myself, which made me like my neighbour. I real-ized with surprise that jokes are humble wonders which help you cope with life's problems; like getting yourself out of bed and giving you courage to repair this muddled world, which is the purpose of our life on earth.

So here's a little yiddisher humour to stop you getting too serious about that perennial worry, sex, because hardly any of us get it right and even then not for long. A tired old Jewish woman walks home from the textile factory. At the corner a flasher leaps out and flings open his overcoat, revealing all. She goes up to him and peers intently. He trembles in anticipation. 'Is that what you call a lining?'

And here's another. Greenland melts and the Jewish suburb of Golders Green will be under six feet of freezing water. People pray in panic all over the place. But the rabbi says severely before the Ark, 'Lord, it's going to be difficult living under six feet of ice water.'

Attaboy, attarabbi! Don't panic despite the Greenland glaciers. As the late Rabbi Hugo Gryn used to tell me, 'In Auschwitz, you could even live without bread for a very short while, but you couldn't live a day without hope.' And perhaps black humour too!

Is religion a good thing? – a problem for Godseekers

Not a nice question, but we can't ignore it because recently it's been a factor in so many assassinations and land grabbings. It's caused so many refugees and de-stabilized so many regimes. It could destabilize the Holy Land, Iran and Iraq, just as it has done Northern Ireland and Bosnia.

My mother thought it wasn't a good thing. She didn't want me to become a rabbi. She called clerics crows and loathed black beards. This led to a family row, and I told her that if I didn't become a rabbi, I'd go east, and come back as a holy man with a begging bowl. I won.

To soften her up, I took her to hear a rabbi talking about how Judaism can turn a house into a home, a kitchen table into an altar and even tragedy into laughter. All she said was, 'He would say that, wouldn't he?'

Perhaps she was right. Listing our own religious virtues is easy. Locating God in others is the test. Here's my experience!

I dived into a railway coach packed with Muslim guest workers going home to Morocco. An elder politely asked me who I was. I told him straight that I was a Jewish rabbi and got frightened as he pointed a parcel at me, 'Eat this baguette, rabbi,' he said. 'It's kosher.' I was ashamed of my paranoia.

I also want to testify how honourable the Muslims I met were when I was setting up a Jewish Christian Muslim trialogue in Europe. Their word really was their bond, though they had more to lose than I did.

But the greatest antagonisms can occur within religions, not between them. Though we unite in emergencies, Jews can often act like one big unhappy family. I want to appreciate the goodness of the very traditional Jews who are at the other end of the religious spectrum from me.

When I visited my mother and aunt in their old people's home, I admired the way the traditional schoolchildren chatted with the oldies every week, so they didn't feel excluded. The youngsters were an example to me.

I was recently examined by a hospital doctor who wore the traditional Jewish skull-cap. What would he make of my liberal lifestyle? But he called me 'Rabbi' politely and I was pleasantly surprised by his concern and courtesy. Paranoia again!

So our task is to witness to God in each other. It's the only way from paranoia to trust.

These words are sometimes said against Jews of my ilk.

Question:
Who do Jews pray to?

Answers:
The traditionalists pray to the God of the rabbis.
The trendy to Almighty God.
And Jews like me – to whom it may concern.
They have a point.

I'd better stop before I get crazed with tolerance and drunk with liberalism.

The positive consequences of religious experience

These are what I and people I know or knew got out of religious experiences: the more or less immediate after-effects.

The glow

You feel a *pure* glow after stepping into that other dimension. It is clearest after doing a good deed on impulse, or after performing or participating in a simple ritual such as lighting the Sabbath candles, or taking Communion, or joining together with a small congregation, or being the congregation of one at Evensong. (This is true for me. For you there may be different turn-ons.)

I have said *pure* because it comes most easily when it is not contaminated by a demonstration of power, nor forms part of the numbers game, nor part of a propaganda exercise or some other 'putting on the style' – as when the ritual is done not just as an expression of the piety you feel but as a demonstration of the piety others don't – as at some funerals. The glow doesn't last long, but its memory stays with you as long as you cherish it. The biggest turn-off for me was when I witnessed 30 priests concelebrating Mass; the numbers game but in holy form.

Heaven is not a place but another dimension which works like gravity; an invisible power that lifts us towards itself if we consent to its working on us. Heaven is already present to us in glimpses in this life. The glow I have mentioned is a sign that we have invested a small part of ourselves in it. Enjoy it!

Heaven on earth

Some think of heaven in personal terms, while some think of it as a place or a state of consciousness. You can think of it in any way you like; the test for me is 'by their fruits ye shall know them' or more prosaically 'the proof of the pudding is in the eating'. It is easy to confuse a journey to heaven with the after-effects of a snort of cannabis. If heaven, or whatever, makes you kinder and more honest *to* yourself *about* yourself, then you're on the right track. If it makes you manipulative and bullying and evasive, then you're on the wrong road. How to deal with it? Have it out with God, X, Jesus, your soul, your Guardian Angel, Fred or your Friend in High Places. Don't get too upset! Remember that narrow is the gate which gets you to what you want – it's not the broad and obvious path.

I thought of God in personal terms because, when I was at Oxford and discovered God, I was very much alone. I had great difficulty making relationships. I did not use the images of Father or Mother in my prayers because, though they loved me, their love was pretty manipulative, and I wasn't sure if I loved them. In fact my flirtation with Christianity was a way of rejecting them, and they knew it. Anyway, I didn't want to project my family problems onto the cosmos, so I didn't use parental figures in prayer. What I wanted desperately was friends, with an erotic dimension if that was possible – it wasn't, it was illegal. So the best I could get was a spiritual friend and that was how my Friend in High Places emerged into my consciousness.

At the beginning I didn't know if he was just a bit of wish-fulfilment whose reason for existence would disappear after my first satisfactory romp in the hay. I had it and he didn't disappear; in fact I needed him then more than ever. I shrieked for his assistance and advice!

After 50 years and more he's still around. He guides me into soul country and I call him Fred.

He's a composite of the brother I never had and the lover I hadn't yet met: there are selected bits of Jesus in him and saintly Jewish refugees I've known, and the ordinary people I've met – German, Jewish, Russian and Dutch – who, when the test came in the Holocaust, loved goodness with all their heart and soul and might, and proved it by offering their lives for others. He's also both of us at our best – we've become more like each other over the years (I hope!).

I'm going to stop because this might all sound appallingly sentimental and delusional. I can understand someone like Professor Dawkins (author of *The God Delusion*) having conniptions. It's like celestial Regency romances. It's true that religion of the sentimental personal type can get very close to slop, but it is also the firmest fearless support we have in life. A curious mixture – I agree. That is why it is so necessary to be honest to oneself about oneself – as I've said before.

Friendship

All serious committed friendships require an investment of time and attention, and the heavenly sort is no different from the worldly sort. At first there is indeed a lot of projection but, as time goes by, provided you have deepened your knowledge and familiarity with your Friend or Whatever, you discover more and more how he looks at things, and without realizing it you absorb it. You grow together.

Worries and the supernatural

I wake up in the morning beset by silly worries chasing each other round my mind. Like returning home four times yesterday searching for my diary. It's in the fridge! My understanding doctor suggests a mild dose of anti-stress tablets (anti-depressants) which he'll monitor. Having survived analysis, I used to be snooty about medical short-cuts; but being 80, I haven't time for dream delving. In any case, God must have created pharmaceuticals too. They help – in conjunction with hot chocolate and romantic bedtime reading.

Many of you readers and listeners are beset with worries – you've told me so – mostly caused by the credit crunch. Shaky pensions, repossessed homes, redundancy and dodgy banking have increased our insecurity, and there's climate change, and new bugs, and inflated egos playing with atomic bombs.

But that's enough moaning! Here are some helpful tips – all personally tested.

Here's a tough one which works. I force myself to recall pictures of refugees in Sri Lanka and starving children in Africa. They put my own woes in perspective. Feeling ashamed of myself, I clumsily try to begin to clean up the world, starting with my clogged electric razor. There's a lot of sanity in small chores. Even more important in stress times, we have to go easy with people around us, especially our spouses and partners. However much we've lost, sincere compliments, kisses and apologies cost nothing yet mean more than we realize. This response might not seem natural when we ourselves feel bitter. Well, it isn't natural – it's more than natural, it's supernatural, which is what religion is about.

I even ask my friend God what I can do for him. 'Give me your worries,' he says, 'I've got everything else.' So mentally I pray them over to him – which helps release them from me. 'Worries lying around are dangerous stuff,' he says. 'They fester into self-pity and anger and fasten onto any scapegoat around.'

I learned to worry from my pious persecuted granny who took me to the seaside. On the beach she shrieked warnings like, 'Eels in the sand will gobble you.' And then, 'Darling, wear a sunhat on your sunhat or you'll get sunstroke like grandpa!' 'Such a worrier,' she whispers to the next deckchair. She then spits three times in my direction to confuse any evil spirits. She certainly confused me. Perhaps that's why, 75 years later, I need to go to the doctor for tablets . . .

Parachuted into Gentile homes

Here's my ha'pennyworth contribution to the great religious debate on schools. Not having children, my own childhood is my example. I was sent to a traditional religion school after state school ended to keep me off the streets. There I was taught that 'the Jew does this' or 'the Jew believes that'. But I didn't believe in the Jew because I'd never met him – only ordinary confused Jews trying to piece together piety with modern London reality.

During the Second World War, I was extracted from my Jewish ghetto and parachuted as an evacuee into one Gentile home after another. I insisted on staying for Christian prayers and religious instruction, and I summoned up courage to ask our teacher why he believed in puzzling miracles. He banged his fist, shouting, 'They're true because they're true.' After that, I kept my big mouth shut, but I wasn't biased – I was puzzled by Jewish miracles as well as non-Jewish ones.

I felt for this Jewish youngster after his first religion class who was asked by his proud parents what he'd learned. 'How a shiny comet landed on earth,' he answered glibly, 'and little striped men wearing skullcaps descended and parted the Red Sea till the Israelites crossed over.' 'Is that what they taught you?' asked his horrified parents. 'Not exactly,' sighed the boy, 'but you wouldn't believe a word of what they really taught us.' How true! Why do adults unload onto children what they don't believe themselves?

I've just been faced by two related problems. At a continental clerical meeting we were asked, 'What values should we instil into the younger generation?' Some said courage, and one punctuality. But many youngsters don't want the old generation's hand-me-downs; they want help to examine their own life experience honestly and to try to work out their own values.

The second was about the growth in faith schools. I'm sympathetic because our souls need education but I worry lest they turn into partisan or class schools with too easy answers. So I think they ought to provide places for a sizeable minority of children of other faiths and none. By respecting their spiritual needs, pupils, teachers and parents will teach themselves what pluralism means in practice and what it requires from all of us.

It will be most demanding on teachers, though the present system's pretty tough too.

'Mummy, mummy,' a son sobs, 'I don't want to go to school today. The children laugh at me, the teachers despise me – and they're all anti-Semites.'

'But, darling, you must, you must,' said his mother desperately.

'But why, why, why?' shrieked her son, clutching her.

'Because my baby,' she said sadly, wringing her hands, 'you're their headmaster.'

Chapter 5

The Holocaust at War

A big black lump

The Holocaust and the fashionable anti-Semitism of the 1930s were like great black lumps on my spiritual journey. How many of the prayers which must have been said in the cattle trucks taking their cargo of human misery to the concentration camps were answered in any way we can understand? So why pray?

And where was God in the tragedy? Was he dozing, sleeping, drunk or being 'discreet'? Why bother with him? 'Shall not the Lord of Justice do justice?'

I have never answered the problem of evil – no one can. But meeting hitch-hikers fleeing Europe and all it stood for, and meditating in places of worship beside former concentration camps, I got glimmers of understanding. And those glimmers and glimpses threw the questions I asked back at me; I knew enough to work out what small steps I, not others, had to take.

Therefore the following pages.

I could not have carried on my Godsearch, dear Godseeker, without these glimmers and glimpses. So I pass them on to you.

One glimpse was very important for me. In a south German church by some railway lines leading to a former labour or concentration camp, I had the following conversation with God – I was very angry!

Me: 'Where were you during the prayers which were said in those cattle trucks of human misery?'

NO ANSWER

Me: 'Were you drunk or dozing? Would it have hurt you so much to take a hand?'

NO ANSWER

Me: 'But you've got no hands – so you're useless!'

As I go through the door, raging within me, my inner voice answers.

Him: 'You're the only hands I've got in this world – over to you!'

Me: 'I've no answer, but I now know the next step for me.'

This made some sense.

Armistice thoughts

I was enrolled in infant school in 1935 and shortly afterwards came the most awesome experience of my young life. We children were all assembled in the hall and, on the eleventh hour of the eleventh day of the eleventh month, the whole school fell silent. Two teachers were crying and the solemnity was such we children didn't even fidget. I held myself rigidly to attention as my father, who had served in the Royal Flying Corps, had taught me. That silence marked the moment when the guns and killing had stopped and there was silence along the whole western front. Thank God, we had won. As in the Second World War, we nearly didn't.

Every village and borough in the country has a memorial to commemorate the suffering and heroism of the men and women who fought in that war – the first total war we had ever known. Rediscover it and read it with the children of your family. That is the least we owe to those who suffered it most.

It was supposed to be the war to end all wars, but it wasn't. I studied this period in history at Oxford and still do not know why we went to war, how we won the war but lost the peace, and why another war, a worse war, had to be fought all over again. Whose fault was that? The politicians, the jingo press, the madness propaganda, the nationalism, or the tribalism that made us drunk?

Years later I asked a congregant, a refugee from Germany who had become British in the Nazi period, what he thought. His face was iron. 'Rabbi Blue,' he said, 'if you had seen the children in Berlin with TB and rickets starving after the war, as I did, you would know how much love it would need to exorcise the bitterness. With all respect to your faith and calling, Rabbi, religion couldn't provide it. Every army in that terrible time was blessed by some religious establishment or other. That is why I so rarely come to your services.'

After the First World War ended, the world became even madder. Bankers jumped off skyscrapers in New York, hungry miners marched on London, and Hitler discovered a scapegoat, a minority made to order, which absolved everyone else of responsibility. On the 9th and 10th of November 1938, the synagogues of Germany were set on fire. Some religious stalwarts protested, some walked on the other side – it wasn't their concern; some said nothing.

Once again every army in the Second World War was blessed by some religious establishment or other – good, evil and in-between.

Which is why I am cautious about religious structures and rely so much on Fred Direct.

A cabalist answer to the creation of evil

The Jewish cabalists said that, when God created the universe, he withdrew from part of his own being so that his creatures could inhabit an empty space and a void. This empty space and void, called 'tohu and bohu', is mentioned at the beginning of the creation story, and it has to be a void so that in it his creatures such as you and I could enjoy his greatest gift of all, which is freedom. This is the price we pay. With that freedom we could accept or reject him and his goodness.

But in that empty space God left sparks of himself, even in the darkest parts of it. And it is our duty in life to release those divine sparks and reunite them with him. That means speaking practically, not mystically, that we somehow have to bring good out of evil and hope out of horror.

Can hope ever come out of the children who went up in the smoke of the gas chambers? From the kids who got caught up and killed in the world's hotspots, the babies dying from malnutrition and AIDS in Africa?

We must try, so that another generation of children will say, 'We live because people learned from their deaths.' So that they became more responsible for each other and especially to the young and defenceless. So that we understand more about those who kill and harm. Is it in their nature or nurture or a sick society? Could a gene ever cure it?

'The evil inclination exists in all human beings,' said the rabbis. What form does it take in each one of us, and how do we overcome it?

You need courage to ask yourself such a question. It is the frontier that separates soft religion from the hard stuff. Be brave!

A black lump within me

The Spirit made me lighter as I've said. But within me lay the black lump, the cancer of the Holocaust. Could all the lightness of religion lift that with its anger, bitterness, fear and hatred?

Eventually, yes, though a bit of it remains. Here's how a part of it at least was laid to rest.

During the Second World War, I took refuge in semi-heated public libraries until closing time, reading anything and everything.

That's how I stumbled across this sentence by Nietzsche, the German philosopher who fascinated Hitler. 'Don't gaze too long into the abyss,' he wrote, 'lest the abyss gaze into you.' I knew what he meant. The horror of the Holocaust, its sadism and its madness, had gazed into me even before the war, though I lived in safe England which actually didn't feel that safe. I remember anti-Semitic insults daubed on Jewish streets, 'Perish Judah' scrawled on synagogues, and my father planning my route home from school through Jewish streets so I didn't get roughed up.

The horror intensified as the refugees from the Nazis arrived in London's poor Jewish East End, each with a more terrifying tale to tell. That was when my nightmares began. And that is why, 70 years later, I still cannot bring myself to visit Auschwitz, Belsen or Birkenau, or watch Anne Frank on TV. I was so sure Britain would be invaded and I'd also end up in a gas chamber.

The first things the Holocaust collapsed were my comforting childhood beliefs. So many prayers must have been said in the trucks to the camps. How many had been answered in any way I could understand – so why pray? And where was God in that increasing horror? Was he dozing, drunk or just couldn't be bothered? So I gave up this useless God and marched with the Reds instead.

The abyss also collapsed my belief in myself. A fascist band came marching down the street. My mother thrust me into a doorway to protect me. I remember secretly wanting to join them and play a fascist drum myself. I was fed up with being a persecuted Jew. I wanted to be on the winning side for a change. Perhaps there was a bit of a Nazi in me. Perhaps there's a bit in most of us – in high clerics and low crooks. It's safer to acknowledge it.

The abyss Nietzsche talked about questioned me ever more closely. Later on, the question began to take this form. 'What would you have done', it said, 'if the Nazis had only shot gypsies, tortured gays and imprisoned liberals, but had left Jews alone, and you were a rabbi in Berlin? Would you have sacrificed your career, or would you have looked the other way.'

I don't know; but sometimes I still torture myself with guilt for a situation I never had to face, thank God!

After the war I had to cross into Germany, a country I'd always avoided because it was a Jewish charnel house; the abyss I feared. But there a strange thing happened. The abyss seemed to turn inside out – a common experience when we ask God's help to confront our fears. I even began to see little lights of self-sacrifice and love shining in it; the more touching because they came from the ordinary people I met as I hitch-hiked across the ruins of the Third Reich, both atheists and believers.

A woman returned to her Berlin flat in 1943. 'Get out, get out,' whispered the concierge, 'the Gestapo have come.' The woman tore off her Jewish badge and walked the streets in despair, finally knocking on the door of a schoolfriend of long ago. The friend gasped but, instead of calling the police, she telephoned a bureau for bombed-out people to get her old friend a new Aryan identity. That was the price of friendship in those times.

And there was the man in the train who asked me to reunite him with his daughter. When the synagogues were torched in 1938, he had tried to put out the flames. A friend warned him to make his peace with the Party for the sake of his wife and children. So he had joined the Party, and now his daughter wouldn't speak to him. 'Tell her how bad it was at that time,' he said urgently, 'she might believe you.' Which I did. Would I have risked my family to put out the flames?

In a gay bar, I listen to stories of hidden friends saved from torture in that dark time. Would I have walked by on the other side?

I remember Rabbi Leo Baeck who, in September 1939, hurried back to Germany. His duty lay with his shattered congregation.

I remember a Jewish doctor urging an elderly patient to vote in the new democratic election. 'Frau Dr,' he said, 'I only voted once before, and look at the suffering I caused, especially to you who have been so good to me. I am too stupid to vote.'

And there was the pastor who issued baptismal certificates to delay deportation, and the Gentile wives of Jewish husbands who demonstrated outside Gestapo offices.

Here are some lessons I learned from my visit to Germany. Some of the angry questions I hurled at God boomeranged back at me. Why had he not taken a hand in that terrible time? Would I have taken a hand if I'd been a rabbi in Berlin in the Nazi time and Hitler had only murdered gays, liberals and gypsies but left Jews alone? I didn't know.

I learned from the Holocaust to beware of unpurified nationalism. Love your country and your culture, but don't try to love your own more by loving others less. That way lies murder – whether it's the Balkans, the Holy Land, Northern Ireland, the Congo – wherever.

I no longer cared if God was all powerful or all anything. It was enough to watch his goodness at work transfiguring people.

As I returned to England, the words of Nietzsche were replaced by the words of the agnostic Roman Emperor Marcus Aurelius whom I'd also bumped into in those wartime libraries. 'I've known the nature of the good,' he wrote, 'and saw that it was beautiful. I've known the nature of evil and saw it was ugly.'

I can only add, 'Me too!'

My unofficial saints helped me to take my first small steps out of my prison of anger and hate: their lights were my guiding stars.

Chapter 6

The Hidden Problems of Religious Experience

Introduction

'I lost good friends by praying for them . . .'

After my Quaker experience, I was on a high. I'd got it. (I'd work out what 'it' was later.)

But then inevitably I tripped up over hidden problems. Silence, which should have been a delight, was a struggle; I needed to know not just the Bible, rites, rituals and creeds, but also that slippery subject of study – myself! It was perilously easy to project my own limitations onto the cosmos.

Another puzzle – friends and relations preferred me as I was 'before', not 'after' my inner illumination. Alas, my light did not show clearly to my nearest and dearest. I lost good friends by praying for them – the ungrateful hinnies!

A problem

A real problem for Godseekers like us is the seemingly insubstantial, see-through nature of what we are seeking, and this had better be faced head on and early on in our search. Religious experiences, spiritual states, God, angels, visions, and spirituality itself, do not have the material solidity or sensual reassurance of things that the material part of us craves. Liquefying blood, dancing Madonnas, holy cities, walls, ruins, bones, the geographical location of Eden, mysterious healings, divine names in aubergines, and heaven on earth, would surely 'prove' the existence of the spiritual, and we wouldn't have to bother about doubt, belief and the struggle between different types of truth. We could just get on with the religious job, whatever that is.

But our situation is not that simple. We human beings are a complex mixture of animal and angel, say the psalms. Like our fellow animals, what is sensual is real but, like the angels, we are also able to give reality to what is beyond the senses – even if only just. Perhaps our religious job is bringing the two realities together; not to avoid the problem by evasion or trying to pretend the problem doesn't exist.

Many thinkers on spirituality gravitate towards the word 'gravity' because that suggests a universal power and strength we cannot see but whose effects we can feel with a quiet force which can pull our sensual life with its needs and delights into an unexpected trajectory like a magnet.

Having felt these pulls (like you), though I cannot prove (or dis-prove) the Divine, I still feel their effects, and their results on me and on others. My life experience makes me trust them. I prefer the word 'trust', because I am not good at belief.

An example! Like many Godseekers, I do not feel that this world is my home. It is not a bad place. I enjoy it in parts, and I certainly don't want to leave it yet, but it doesn't feel like home; home for me is not another place but another dimension.

I realized my metaphysical situation at a Spanish airport in the height of the tourist season. Waiting at Departures, I found myself surrounded by a confused crowd of German tourists who, in bad Spanish, asked me to direct them to their buses and taxis. They'd fastened onto me because I looked dark, dishevelled and native. I replied to them in even worse German (childhood Yiddish really) that I was also only a tourist, 'a bloody foreigner' like them. After they'd gone, I pondered my answer. I'd said more than I realized. I wasn't just a foreigner in Spain, but in this world, here on a temporary tourist visa.

I imagined this world as a kind of departure lounge; I'd make myself as comfortable as possible in it, make acquaintances, try to make myself useful, and exit when my flight was called – the time of which I couldn't completely control. I was in a waiting-room or, as the medieval rabbis said, a passage to another dimension beyond space and time, and therefore beyond my imagination.

A warning! Do not try to create false experiences out of desperation, or the need to have something to show. I was in such a situation myself. In medieval literature Godseekers sometimes fluttered their eyelashes to see the unseen. Out of curiosity, I tried it myself. But I was not medieval, and I learned to steer clear of such spiritual vaudeville. No God is less dangerous than a False God. Once again, a lesson from Simone Weil.

How we falsify religion

Dear Godseeker,

It was my doubting but curious mother who asked me the bull's-eye question. 'Lionel,' she said, toying with her hot madras curry cooled down with gin, 'will all that religion you're learning make you nicer?' I was startled into truth. She was honest with me and genuinely interested, so I'd be honest with her. Religion can lure you into many little white lies. 'I don't know,' I said, unwillingly. 'Religion can make you nasty as well as nice, ma, so we'll just have to see, won't we?' We sat in brooding silence. The problem couldn't be brushed under the carpet. The truth shall make you free, not a liar – not even a white one.

Just as God tries to make us in his image, we can't help trying to make him in ours. Read any newspaper of the serious sort, and you'll quickly discover that religion isn't only the answer to problems, it's also part of the problem, and sometimes it's the problem itself. Think of Ireland, Afghanistan, the Holy Land, religious terrorism – wherever you look you'll see the secular and holy in unholy muddle.

Here are some ways religion has gone wrong with me. They seem so obvious and simple, but they can infect not just you or me but entire religions, venerable ones too.

One is the result of spiritual laziness. God is high and we are low. Growing towards God requires sustained effort, which can be exhausting. So why not bring God down to our level instead of raising ourselves to his? It's cosy but dangerous. We make him human-sized and project onto him all our human limitations – our prejudices, our falsifications, our little white lies, our fantasies. We make him the God of our group, our tribe, our class, the big boss. We start to worship ourselves. Megalomania is a constant religious temptation.

There's another problem; less intended, but with the same result. Someone writes to me asking how she or he can share my religious experience. The answer is obvious, isn't it? I tell them I'm a reform Jew, and a member of a north-west London synagogue. I tell her/him also to become a north-west London Jew, and to attend the same synagogue. In other words, I make God suburban with an 0208 telephone number. I confuse local respectability with cosmic truth so that, unless you become like me, you can't share my experience. This is an assumption made in many well-meant sermons and conversions.

Here is an even more deadly error, easy to fall into, which poisons much organized religion. I became aware of it while visiting a girls' school and watching out of the window the groups forming and re-forming in the playground. One skipping group had jelled. Innocently they took turns skipping in pairs. Another girl came up to them, nervously wanting to join in. But they didn't open the circle for her, and a big girl spoke up for the group. 'We don't play with the likes of you,' she said, and looked around triumphantly at her mates, who giggled and tittered at the newcomer who slunk away, a rejected outsider. The rejection had an immediate effect on the skippers; they couldn't stop talking about the rejected girl, and some hurled catcalls after her. Having a common outsider, a common hate object, had drawn them closer together and melded them. They had aborted their religious progress.

Now the task of religion is to make your affection and love ever more inclusive. A baby loves itself and then learns to love its family and then its family's friends. In a good life the circles of love grow ever wider until finally you love your enemies, though this is very hard. Sometimes you reach your limit before that, and it's better to accept that you are no saint and to leave well alone. What you must *not* do is make your love for your own group stronger by withdrawing love from an outsider and even hating her or him. Love then flows backward and turns sour. Once again – you love your own, you love yourself! Who are the outsiders? Class enemies, racial enemies, Jews, gypsies, homos, Martians, anyone who gets in the way of your security, anyone you don't understand and, preferably, anyone who can't hit back. (By the way, it's harder to like people than to love them.)

It's an easy mistake. That is why religions have burned, tortured and massacred other religious groups or good atheists or agnostics, and they've all done the same in return if and when they get power, and the result is not heaven but hell!

At the beginning of religious life we want to change everybody else. Later on, we realize how much we have to change ourselves. To change ourselves we have to know ourselves, and this can be frightening and takes a lot of courage – there are so many cans of worms in all of us. We have all been the disloyal friend, the bad neighbour (whom we are supposed to love), the jealous partner, and the untrustworthy child. To change ourselves also takes a lot of time – a lifetime or even more.

'A good person looks after his own soul and other people's bodies,' said the rabbis, 'and with a hypocrite it's the other way round.'

The sages of the Talmud also said, 'Just because you can't finish the work doesn't mean that you shouldn't begin it.'

So take heart. If you take the first step, God comes to meet you, a power comes to help you, and it gets easier as you go along.

I am not citing a textbook but my own experience – this is how it happens to me.

In this hard task, humour can help you.

Preachers like me for example have a special problem with penitence. Hypnotized by our own sermons, we can believe we are God or his clone. This is a danger for would-be mystics. But humour is a good deflator.

In the middle of a preacher's peroration, a worshipper makes for the exit. 'Where are you going?' shouts the angry preacher. 'To get a haircut,' retorts the man. 'You should have thought of that before I began,' says the preacher. 'Before you began, your reverence,' shouts back the man, 'I didn't need one.'

First-rate and third-rate religion

'A rabbi's a rare bird in our pub,' they tell me, and my stock goes up. But as they're connoisseurs of real ale, my stock zooms down when they discover I adulterate my lager with lime.

So they ask me awkward questions like, 'How can you trust religion when it causes trouble everywhere? Look at the Holy Land, look at Iraq.' 'Why go so far?' I ask. 'Look at Northern Ireland. And look at my glass,' I say meanly, 'it's empty and it's your call.' But they're right: it's a scandal which is blowing religious credibility to bits.

After my second glass I become loquacious, telling them that religion comes in different grades, just like real ale, and you need discrimination with it as with everything else. There's first-rate religion, which for me means Anne Frank, Josephine Butler, Titus Brandsma and my granny. But there's the third-rate stuff too, such as manipulative religion, showbiz religion and hate religion. I prefer sincere ethical atheism to that lot. No god can be better than false gods.

When I was a youngster I went in for third-rate ideologies and religions because I was having a hard time with puberty and adolescence, and desperately needed security. I wanted instant answers and reach-me-down belief I didn't have to think through or take responsibility for. I wanted to emote, so I shouted slogans in Marxist processions and sang sticky nationalist songs round campfires.

I was then attracted to know-it-all religious teachers and preachers who had the answer to everything. But after getting my first hundred wrong answers, I retched it all up. Never mind! My foray into fundamentalism has stood me in good stead because I now understand why so much religion goes awry – why some settlers in Gaza believe on rather shaky evidence that that's the place God wants them to settle and why pious suicide bombers want to blow them off it and themselves into paradise.

But as I've got older, my religion's become simpler and humbler. I no longer think that doubt is a disease but something precious which helps us grow up. I don't pray for difficulties to disappear, just for courage to face them. Also, to know God I must know myself because he's within me.

I've also found my own humility through humour, of which there isn't much in scripture. When I'm drunk on clericalism I remember the story of an old boy in the front row of the synagogue who snored his way through the sermon. 'Shake him!' the preacher told the beadle. 'Shake him yourself, your reverence,' he snorted, 'seeing as you put him to sleep.'

A joke can deflate you more efficiently than an hour on your knees.

A note on doubt

Dear Godseeker,

Don't be frightened of doubt. It is neither the devil nor a disease, but a very necessary discipline for spiritual hygiene. Without a healthy dose of it, you won't get to heaven but to cloud cuckoo-land. Learning its lesson is part of the hard work that real religion requires. Beginners don't like it, of course. I didn't myself. Part of me was using religion to sublimate too much adolescent testosterone. Naturally I preferred ecstasies, eyelid fluttering to simulate angels, voices, and an awful lot of kitsch – on the same level as the devotional junk statuettes in play-safe places of worship, chestnut-haired Jesus cuties and tearful blond Aryan Madonnas (both smiling sadly through tears), holy walls, and insipid souvenirs of Jerusalem.

A problem with doubt is natural when your belief is new and precarious and you're worried that, if you don't believe the lot (though a lot is quite unbelievable), the whole edifice will come tumbling down. When one sect persecutes another, it is not the mark of faith but of doubt. When groups burn or behead their opponents, it is because they are trying to burn or behead the doubt in themselves.

My own advice is not to get panicky. Religious experience is tougher than you give it credit for. It can bear the weight of your life. You only realize how strong it is when you decide you've had enough of it and try to delete it from your mind. It doesn't delete!

Change, yes, but delete, no. Of course clerics tell you that you can't pick 'n mix religion. But in my experience everyone does just that; some people have the courage to admit it, while others attribute such dastardly behaviour only to their opponents. As one of my converts to Judaism remarked, 'They would say that, wouldn't they!' Sooner or later you must separate what Anne Ridler called 'the junk and treasure of an ancient creed'.

The rabbis said some good things about doubt – mind you, they said something good and bad about everything in their endless disputations. 'If only they would forsake Me, but keep my commandments,' says God. And the rabbis, 'When someone comes along to ask your help, don't say God will help you, but act as if there were no God, as if he didn't exist.'

To these I would add a more modern remark – to know God, you also have to know yourself: the two types of knowledge must go hand in hand. Since the Kingdom of Heaven is within us, if we try to increase our knowledge of God without increasing our knowledge of ourselves, we project our limitations onto the cosmos and may end up worshipping them.

I learned from my teacher, Rabbi Dr Leo Baeck. I had some tutorials from him when I started to study for the rabbinate, though they were more like courteous conversations. I could never forget that he had had one of the greatest and most difficult jobs in the world. He had become a Chief Rabbi in Germany just as Hitler came to power. He had to oversee the dissolution and death of one of the most cultured Jewish communities ever. He had returned to Berlin in haste just as the war was about to break out at the beginning of September 1939, just as anyone with sense was frantically trying to leave it. He rushed there from London because he knew war was imminent and he had to cross the border before it was closed – he had to look after the remnants of his once great community who couldn't leave – the old, the sick, those without the influence or money to get a visa (not many countries would open the door to Jewish refugees), those looking after dependants who were too feeble to leave. Eventually he was imprisoned in Theresienstadt and escaped the fatal journey to Auschwitz by a fluke of fate. When Theresienstadt was liberated by the Russians, who handed the guards over to the prisoners, it was Baeck who stopped the prisoners from killing the guards, insisting on their right to a fair trial. He was one of the first rabbis to return to Germany after the war. He remained a German Jewish Liberal – the last of an endangered species.

I had the following conversation with him not long before he died. 'Mr Blue,' he enquired, 'where are you taking your holiday?' 'I don't know,' I replied, 'I might visit a friend in an ultra orthodox Jewish seminary or visit other friends I made at Oxford who have become novices at monasteries.' I paused, disconcerted. Had I hurt the old boy's feelings, for he was, as I've said, one of the most liberal rabbis I'd ever met? 'Do you mind, Dr Baeck?' I stammered. 'Mr Blue,' he said, amused, 'please remember that your Judaism is your religious home, it is not your religious prison.'

That is what most people need in an age of pious or atheist fundamentalism – a religious home, not a religious prison. But perhaps they prefer the rigidity of a prison to the freedom of a home – for the latter you have to grow up and take responsibility.

Those words have enabled me to remain in official religion; but I do not feel I am doing the creation a service by suppressing my doubts. A lot of what Marx said about late capitalism is proving only too true, and it was Wilhelm Reich, a radical follower of Freud, who released me from my inner sexual nightmares. Both great men were atheists. I owe a lot to them and I am pleased both Marx and Freud are quoted in the prayer book I edited for my organization.

So don't be frightened of atheists or agnostics: learn from them – yes, even from Professor Richard Dawkins: a lot of what he says is only too true. Honour Marcus Aurelius, Primo Levi, Karl Marx, Sigmund Freud, Dr Magnus Hirschfeld and Wilhelm Reich.

Religiously speaking, I have remained free range, not force-fed battery. Dogmatism comes from fear but, as it says in the Gospels, 'The truth shall make you free'; but freedom does not, of course, make you cosy.

Silence

How do you deal with silence? Is it good for you? Is it anything or just a blank, an emptiness, a waste of time? What do Godseekers find in it, why are they so attracted by it, or say they are? Isn't liturgy enough? And if it is nothing, why do we avoid it? Why do we find it uncomfortable, but why don't we like to admit it? Why, even if we like it, do we find a sense of relief when it's over? Singing out hymns is so much more satisfying – intelligible and energizing!

It certainly brings out some strong and strange reactions. With some fellow rabbis, I retired to a monastery. Jews are a talkative lot, but we decided some silence would be good for us and we would keep at least fifteen hours of it. But ten hours was more than enough: it all ended in bitter rows and recriminations. Late in the night, we marched out of the monastery, piled into cars, and burst into a nearby jolly curry-house where, over beers and madras, we thanked God for not turning us into contemplatives.

So don't get worried if you don't take to the stuff straight away. You can just read about silence instead, or write a doctorate on it.

But it's worth persevering, and I offer my own experience which might help you slip into it more easily. Prayers are not just words but the expression of a friendship, a relationship; and each friendship has its own laws, its own style. You find out what yours is by use. Since it takes two to tango, and no two relationships are quite alike, you not only have to find out what's right for you but also what's right for Fred.

The strangeness of starting up long fixed lengths of silence in a formal place of prayer following a formal service is the same strangeness I find in diving into a swimming pool filled with water but with no other swimmers. It's going unaccompanied into an alien element. If you stifle the extrovert conscious part of yourself, you are making room for the sadness and horrors of your subconscious or apprehension of truths too big to handle and demands you can't possibly fulfil. (Something in us likes to turn God into a sadist.)

Taking a book with you to read is a good way of getting into it bit by bit, inch by inch instead of diving in. Read a bit and let your mind wander a bit. Then, if it wanders into dangerous territory, you can return to the book for another bit. Take it easy! Note the changing light in the windows.

At night, my time for silence, I try to think of all the people awake with me. People in the big hotels, the tourists, people in bars who haven't found a partner for the night. I don't force anything, but a wave of compassion for night people washes over me. I shall seal it with an act of charity in the morning.

You might find that the way to inner peace is stormier than you expect, and funnier.

When I went to a Pilgrim Centre with my Jewish girl friend, Evie, we were asked by some friendly people to join their walk and we accepted. We found ourselves following a wooden cross, silent and shoeless, down a lane to a chapel with a tomb, like something out of the Castle of Otranto or a medieval procession of penitents. I was trembling with fear lest one of my congregants was motoring in the area, and a photo of me appear prominently in next week's Jewish newspaper.

'What embarrassing nonsense this all is. I should be feeding the poor, healing the sick – no, not raising the dead – I'm only a beginner. If I'm in a church, what if a fellow Jew sees me? If I'm in a synagogue, what if a Christian sees me?'

Then you (me) might hit a layer of domestic panic. Have you put the gas out and let the cat in? Where are your (my) keys? Surely you should break off and hurry home as fast as you can.

Then I sit back and remember all the embarrassing moments of my life, mainly sexual.

Then I feel sorry for myself and almost begin to cry.

Then I lean back exhausted and stop trying to be anything or get anywhere. I feel washed out but peaceful and look at another silent worshipper; taking a piggy-back on his piety.

The silence is comforting; there's a message in it for me.

It usually takes me about fifteen to twenty minutes to become silent inside. If you can have a dozen sessions of it, you should know whether spiritual silence is full or empty for you. It's worth finding out, and it requires no more time or effort than learning how to strum a guitar.

The Quakers try to empty their minds to let the Holy Spirit flow in, and this seems very reasonable.

If silence precipitates avoidances and worries, it is worthwhile considering what is so worrying. We're worried if nothing happens to us in the silence no matter how much straining and effort we put into it, in which case there's nothing there and bang goes our religion, Fred, our Friend in High Places, our minimal faith and our inner voice. This must not be allowed, especially if we're religious professionals. Or what happens if some voice does speak to us in the silence and it says things which are too demanding, which we can't possibly fulfil, or which are just bizarre? We wanted God, and we've got him. We're trapped like a trap in a trap.

One sensible way to start with silence is to begin thinking about a real problem in your life, not a false problem which you ought to be concerned with but aren't. I ask Him what He thinks about it, to show me what is packed into it, and what is my next step ahead with it. I need to see my life from His point of view. In chatting together, as it were, we become real to each other and get to know each other. And then affection springs up between us. That's how all friendships deepen, this-worldly or other-worldly. They need an investment of attention and time to talk to each other and begin to like and enjoy each other and then sit in silence holding each other's hand as it were. We need to use each other. Later on we can even joke with each other.

At this stage in my life I no longer go in for long periods of heavy silence: it involves too much obligation for friendship. Instead I'm silent many times for a few minutes. I blow a kiss, as it were. I ask a question, get a moment's insight. Sometimes I comfort Him. The world's so awful, He must be having an even worse time of it than I am since He carries most of the responsibility. In silence (though sometimes out loud if I'm alone) I like to tell Him about my day and how the events of it seemed to me. And about the people I've met. Quite often I begin to see the events in a different kind of way – His way. Sometimes we agree or agree to differ. I often end with a poem or song that says it all – George Herbert's 'The Guest', or Sydney Carter's pop hymn 'One more step ...'

One woman I heard about puts a kitchen towel round her head and turns her scullery into a chapel of whiteness (it must be a clean towel) and silence. Vera von der Heydt, the Jungian analyst and refugee, told me how she sat in silence before an image of Jesus in the Brompton Oratory and watched as the statue sucked into itself all her bitterness and anger – at last she was free! Sometimes a presence sits in a chair beside me as it were, and I lose my fears and anxiety. If all this intimacy sickens you, I completely understand. Obviously I have a very kitschy imagination, though Vera did not. But a spiritual experience need not be an aesthetic one. Silent prayer is so personal we must be true to ourselves.

Many years ago I tried to organize a Jewish retreat on silence. We sat down and organized the programme. There would be an introduction on the Place of Silence in Jewish tradition, followed by a talk on Silence in Jewish Mysticism, followed by Silence in the Talmud, followed by a psychotherapist who would tell us about The Use of Silence in Therapy and Counselling. We were very proud of our programme until we showed it to a Friar friend (Father Gordian OP), who giggled and pointed out that our retreat was so full of *talking* about silence there was no room to *experience* it. It was the most chatty silent retreat he had ever encountered!

Self-knowledge

I repeat, if your religious experience makes you kinder, more generous and more honest to yourself about yourself, then go for it! You're on the right road; it's very likely the real thing. The first two validations – kindness and generosity – are obvious. Self-knowledge is not as obvious and not as immediately enjoyable as the other two, but just as essential – especially if you're experiencing the bliss that the first hint of heaven brings.

This truth came home to me very forcefully after my own exciting experiences with the Quakers and Anglo-Catholics. My religious experiences did not save me from a dark depression and even a half-hearted suicide attempt (the normal cry for help). Religious pep stories usually over-emphasize the difference between 'before' and 'after' – so useful in the advertising world. For most of us, the reality is living with both at the same time, often for a lifetime.

Some weeks after meeting up with the Quakers, my friends threw a dismal 'party' held in my 'honour' to celebrate my non-return to Oxford. At the party, a mousy man uncurled himself from the shadows while I was singing Bessie Smith's 'Down and Out Blues' and brusquely told me to come and see him the following morning at 10 o'clock. Which I did (any port in a storm), and then began my Reichian analysis (six-hour or eight-hour sessions, once, twice, or three times a week for the next year and a half). Wilhelm Reich was Freud's most radical disciple.

I proudly announced to the rest of Balliol that I'd asked Leslie Shepard, my analyst, whether my religion would get analysed away along away with my depressions. (Then I would have a good reason to discontinue the analysis if the going got too tough.) Leslie said that, insofar as my religion was neurotic, it would hopefully go; insofar as it wasn't, it would stay. He could give me no more comfort than that. In the end, the situation was reversed. After finishing my analysis with him, I decided to become a cleric and he moved from Marx to Vedanta.

Incidentally, I also asked him about the relative merits of Freudian and Jungian analysis. Once again, his answer was succinct and convincing. He said they were two different ways to self-understanding. The former was more direct, but the latter was a more interesting ride. He also said the greatest guru of all was life itself.

If God is with us, why do we require self-knowledge?

This was a question I asked myself at the time. The following are my early problems with formal religion and the answers which formed during private meditation in empty churches and chapels.

It is easy to infect the cosmos with your own childhood hang-ups. I have not, for example, used the parent or father-figure in my own construct of God. I am not a parent myself, and my relations with my own parents were too complex and messy to be projected onto the cosmos. In private prayer I prefer to use the word 'friend'; it is the relationship I am best at – with some awful lapses.

I am also cautious about *pietism*. Its practices and repetitions often become compulsive, and the constant use of repetition feels akin to my going back again and again to check up on locks and keys or, as a child, not walking on the cracks between paving stones or touching specific things. Once again, self-knowledge was important. Otherwise it is easy to deify one's limitations and neuroses. In the end one can even worship them.

I also began to realize that many of the neurotic patterns did not come from me but were embedded in formal religion itself. Although Religion (the capital is important) aimed rightly at truth, it was not good at honesty. It was good at love, but not nearly as good at sex, the inconvenient practicalities of which it often ignored. My case was especially difficult being homosexual. The official hard line didn't fit and, what is worse, couldn't even be spoken about (one could only talk about 'that' to a convenient mythical 'friend' and even then only in whispers).

It was also difficult getting straight talk on sublimation. The difficulty here was that 'one size fits all' doesn't work. Some could easily transfer sexual energy into spiritual energy. Others couldn't and, instead of arriving in heaven, hit the bottle or mammoth depressions. This led to deviousness and avoidance, and infected the important things such people had to say.

Sooner or later the journey inside yourself can't be avoided because, below the neurotics which are part of our human situation, there is God's image imprinted within us.

Self-knowledge can be very hard to handle and not many spiritual types can cope with Freud; Jung is an easier ride. I discussed this with the only German pastor I know who is a Freudian. The best way to assimilate him is to start with Auden's 'In Memory of Sigmund Freud' – you face the truth head on but in a friendly manner. Religion is always wriggling out of uncomfortable truths. Marxism did the same.

The after-effects of religious experience

Yes, you do get nicer, but in patches. Exasperated friends tell you you're inconsistent; and they're right. You may feel badly used and persecuted like so many holy hermits, saints and rabbis before you. Or perhaps you try to bluff it out. Yet part of you has the awful feeling that they're right. Don't worry about it. You can't at this stage of the game be anything else. Why so? Well, probably a little bit of you has gone ahead of yourself and the rest of you hasn't yet caught up. That's why you're inconsistent and your behaviour, erratic, tender, sweet and generous one moment, then arrogant, assertive and superior the next.

How long is it going to take the rest of you to catch up? Possibly a lifetime! So take it easy. Recognize the problem and ask X/Fred/ You Know Who to help sort it out. 'Don't take it too hard, dearie!' as my streetwise friend Bertie used to advise me in Amsterdam when I was caught up in closely related physical and metaphysical muddles. You're working and living from two centres, that's all. I found it very similar to how I felt after giving up chain-smoking – gentle, dreamy and sweet one moment, then suddenly I'd change and bite someone's head off. Getting unhooked from smoking took me three months. Getting unhooked from this rat-race world and my own past could take more than a lifetime. Humour is helpful, as are a lot of jokes. Here's a neat way to deal with the situation. Just agree with your opponents sweetly, which will disconcert them. You can be very uppish and domineering in an over-humble sort of way. 'You pray to him in your way, and I'll pray to Him in His.'

Religion can make you very nasty as well as nice, as I eventually admitted to my mother. This, I think, comes from insecurity. You haven't got your 'act' together, that's all – integrating the secular and the spiritual parts of you. My flatmate at Oxford told me that I became quite impossible after my 'conversion'. And he meant it; he moved out the following term. Of course I felt persecuted, like all God's saints, but later on I agreed with him. 'I didn't mind too much,' he said, 'when you stained my books with pickled herring or chocolate, or prayed for me audibly when I came back from a party, but it was that smug forgiving look on your face I couldn't stand. I just wanted to hit it.'

We came together again after I became less pious.

A similar thing happened when I decided to become a rabbi and my mother told my father not to garden on the Sabbath so as not to disturb my spiritual sensibilities. Now my father worked all week in a noisy, steamy factory (it was how I pictured hell), but he had the soul of a countryman and rejoiced in growing vegetables for the family, friends and neighbours, and the Sabbath was the only day he could become the countryman he really was. But he was a good-natured soul and agreed miserably that God, through little Lionel, had spoken. My grandfather had to smoke his pipe in the loo on the Sabbath for the same reason.

This went on for some time, and even I was getting uneasy. Finally Fred took a hand and told me in prayer that if I tried to use him in this way he would break my bloody neck. Faced with this order from on high I apologized and desisted. A rabbinic saying clinched the matter: 'A pious man cares for his own soul and other people's bodies. With a hypocrite, it's vice versa'.

Nastiness is often an accompaniment to undigested piety. You persecute others because they stand for the disbelief inside you that you don't know how to deal with. This is the time when you realize that you can't solve all your problems yourself; you need a teacher and guide through this unfamiliar spiritual terrain. But it's not easy to find one, though there are quite a lot about and you probably bump into them daily. But you don't see them because they're not what you expect. There are no degrees and doctorates in generosity or humility. BA can stand for 'Bastard!' as well as your graduation.

Another problem concerns not belief in God but belief in yourself and in your own experience. Don't underrate either. I used to get worried that I was saying more in my sermons than I was entitled to say. Was I a self-inflated fraud or self-hypnotized phoney? Possibly a bit of both – but there's something else too. And it's that 'something else' which is the important bit. In your sermon, you might have said something wiser than you really knew. In religion, some deeper insights do well up from the depths you didn't know you had. One part of you has gone forward from the rest of you – that's all.

Another thing that can come with religious experience is a dose of megalomania. I was so surprised that anything happened at all that, in my first experiences of the reality of dimensions beyond the senses, I tried to expand what I actually experienced because of my own unsureness and insecurity. So I compensated by becoming over-certain and dogmatic. I'd had a taste of the spirit, a seeming scrap of conversation with Fred – and now I knew what Fred/God had for breakfast. Like most human beings, once again I wanted material support for spiritual realities.

What did I get out of prayer and religious experience? A conviction about my next step ahead and some courage to take it. These were the daily bread of life. I didn't know whether Fred was eternal or all-powerful or, indeed, all-anything, or a mere guide; and it didn't really matter – he was the goodness that dwelt in me, and that was enough.

Like Marcus Aurelius, I had seen the nature of good and knew that it was beautiful, and I had seen the nature of evil and knew that it was ugly. What I knew, and what Marcus Aurelius may not have known, was that this spirit of goodness was more than an idea or an ideal or conscience, it had all the richness and complexity of personality and more. I could have an affair with it, I could make love to it. It was the baby I cared for, my friend in high places. It was not for putting on the style, it was truth. I began to understand what Thérèse of Lisieux meant by writing that the only thing she wanted was the truth. Or how Edith Stein, after reading Teresa of Ávila, had exclaimed, 'This is the truth' and started on her journey as a nun on a path which eventually led to her death in Auschwitz.

Chapter 7

Unofficial Seminaries and Teachers

Introduction

Some of my unofficial seminaries and teachers:

Seminaries

- Meditating on arrivals and departures at London stations.
- Hospital waiting-rooms.
- Kibbitzing bridge games.
- Conversing with the dead at cemeteries.
- Mixed faith retreats.
- Peculiar pilgrimages.
- Gay sauna in Amsterdam.
- Hitchhiking 'away from here'.
- Bars and churches in Germany.

Teachers

- A cabalist.
- A hedgerow worker priest.
- Fr Gordian Marshall OP.
- Leslie Shepard – Reichian analyst and vedantist.
- The brave and the conformists in Holocaust Germany.
- Rabbi Dr Leo Baeck.
- Rabbi Dr Wernher Vanderzyl.

- Discalced Carmelites.
- Tante Tina from the sauna.
- My parents – who put up with a lot.
- Joanna Mary Hughes – who put up with even more!
- Hospital staff (nurses, consultants, cleaners and tea ladies).
- My own life experience.

A lesson I had to teach myself

Like many adolescents, I was a mess and nobody wanted to listen. My parents being bourgeois just said, 'Yes, yes, dear – pass the sprouts.' My revolutionary comrades also didn't listen, just saying it was the fault of the class struggle.

After falling into religion, I tried again with assorted clergy. A Jewish minister said being gay was a Gentile problem which didn't affect Jews – which left me nowhere. Some Christian ministers recommended sublimation in a monastery, though a nunnery might have been more relevant. They were even more confused about sex than I was.

My breakdown occurred as expected and I ended up on an analyst's couch in King's Cross. I was amazed when he asked me to tell him how the world seemed to me and listened to my answer.

Eventually I decided to become a cleric myself and at my seminary learned how to talk the hind legs off a donkey – but 'listening' I had to teach myself.

I visit a hospital. 'How well you look this morning,' I babble to a patient. He knows he is not looking well, but I carry on babbling because my religion is still at the 'All things bright and beautiful' stage, and I can't cope with the pain in his eyes. He lets me off the hook and I go away knowing he has ministered to me, not me to him.

I learned that words *cover* meaning as well as *convey* it. A man comes to see me about a theological question. We discuss it every which way. As he exits, he says, 'By the way, Rabbi . . .' We start all over again, but this time we don't talk about theology but about his life.

I attend a meeting about Jerusalem. People justify, testify, exhort and monologue, attacking their opponents' hang-ups and defending their own. It's like a madhouse. They daren't listen because then they might understand and feel the burning injustice among the Palestinians and the historic insecurity of all Jews and the 'backs to the sea' insecurity of the Israelis. Old-fashioned bombs, booms and bangs aren't signs of strength but lack of an inclusive vision – desperation even.

Today try to listen, really listen – not just to the words people utter but to what lies behind their words. It isn't comfortable because then you begin to feel their pain. Real listening requires your heart and mind – not just your ears. Even trained people shrink from it.

Two old friends bump into each other in Harley Street. 'I can't stay,' says Hymie, 'I'm already late for my analyst.' 'Why worry?' says Mo, 'after all, she can't start without you.' 'But mine does,' says Hymie. 'She's a cute cookie,' he says admiringly.

A lesson from life experience

I felt for the young hopefuls marooned in an airport on their way to their holiday of a lifetime. Oldies like me can cope better because we were brought up in the blitz. We're able to start up singsongs and sleep spooned against strangers, even if we don't know where they've been.

But it's no use crying over spilt milk, and here are some tips which can at least help you on your return journey if, God forbid, you're again held to ransom. In holiday time vulnerable holiday-makers make tempting targets.

I think the worst rows, when you're returning and imprisoned as I've been in the Departure lounge, aren't even those between you and the powers that be but between you and your nearest and dearest. It took me and my good friends years before we came back from a holiday still speaking.

What happened was simple. All my worries about the work waiting for me back home had hit me even before the farewell hotel barbecue, and trouble at the airport was just the last straw. Like a child, I started blaming everyone around. My friends were around, so I blamed them and they bit my head off because they had their problems too.

My advice – be open! Tell your family and friends what's bugging you and why, and ask them to forgive you in advance. Give yourself a Brownie point for all the clever, unforgivable remarks you *don't* say. Say them to God if you must – that's what he's there for.

Rows aren't always bad, provided you know how to make up. Some people need one before they can make love. Some people row to clear the air, and some to make their partner feel guilty – but that's dodgy. It's neither the time nor the place to say, 'and by the way your hair droppings disgust me'. One clever truth like that can wreck any holiday friendship for ever.

Some practical points: don't be caught on the hop! Bring a fat book with a happy ending to escape into, your pills, a thermos of tea, and a large fruit cake for you and yours. Munching is safer than bad mouthing. Also take a smaller fruit cake for those around you. Doing a little good makes you feel good. Don't drink alcohol, or someone else's bottle of holy water, or get paranoid. Remember – you don't lose passports, you mislay them.

Use the same techniques in hospital waiting-rooms!

By the way, I must stress that making love in an airport would be most unwise. Too many frustrated holidaymakers, bored beyond endurance, would try and tell you how they could do it better and illustrate it graphically. Most embarrassing!

The cabalah changes my life!

I was accepted as a rabbinical student nearly 60 years ago. But where should I train for it? The only reformed rabbinical seminaries in Europe had been burned by the Nazis, there were none in Israel, and they didn't want to send me to America lest I find the holy land in Hollywood and never come back. So I was sent to university to study Hebrew and Aramaic grammar.

There, a university lecturer kindly gave me some lessons outside the syllabus for my spiritual education, and introduced me to Jewish mysticism called cabalah, whose cosmic vistas overwhelmed me. 'Did he know a real cabalist?' I asked. 'Many who called themselves such are self-hypnotized phonies,' he said. Finally he directed me to an old man who lived above a prayer room amid sleazy bars and restaurants.

In his attic, and un-shocked by my modernism, the old boy made me Russian tea. 'What is religion?' I asked. 'The art of giving without strings,' he said tersely.

He didn't mention rites, rituals, theology or cosmology, and I was puzzled by its revolutionary simplicity. In this light, my mother's family was deeply religious, though they didn't think so and neither did I. They didn't belong to a synagogue, only to a burial society, and ma kept three boxes in the larder, two for the traditional division of milk and meat and one forbidden. But granny extended her kosher borscht soup to striking Welsh miners, ma gave her only winter coat to the coughing cleaning woman, and dad his breakfast to a scabby dog.

I used the same cabalistic test at Oxford, where a theology student instructed me in the importance of ecclesiastical orders, creeds and so forth. I only took this strange stuff seriously after I lost my toothbrush while we hitched to the Holy Land. 'Share mine,' he said promptly. Greater love hath no man!

I applied the same test to Britain which had bankrupted itself during the war and lost its empire. Was it still great? The experts said no. The cabalah said yes, very. From Britain had come the Salvation Army and the Samaritans, a Health Service for all, and hospices for decent dying, the voluntary Citizens' Advice Bureau for the bewildered, a profusion of charity shops, free libraries and museums, and teachers who freely took us to those libraries and museums after working hours. Cabalistically speaking, it was an even greater country post-war than pre-war, and I was proud to be part of it.

I stumbled across the evidence of that greatness in an obscure window in Liverpool Cathedral. One panel commemorated a working woman who had washed soiled and infected clothes in her boiler during the cholera epidemic, and another an upper-class lady who had nursed diseased prostitutes from the streets in her own home. I felt awed.

But here's a tale of un-cabalistic giving. A man buys a lavish complete illustrated cookbook. 'It's an anniversary present for my wife,' he tells the admiring check-out girl. 'How wonderful,' says the girl, 'she'll love it!' 'Do you think so?' he smiled thinly, 'she was expecting dinner at the Ritz!'

I heard it, laughed and shivered.

A very awkward woman

I was sorry when I couldn't get another copy of Simone Weil's *Waiting on God* in the bookshop because it's being reprinted (hopefully!). Of all modern writers on spirituality, she is the one who impresses me most, and I regularly re-read her. A lot of spiritual writing strikes me as comfy kitsch, rather like the romances I favour before I get to sleep.

I must say straight away that, though I respect her enormously, I've never liked her. Sometimes she's left me so angry I want to hurl her thoughts out of the window. But then I console myself with the fact that she wouldn't have liked me either, so we were quits. Though born a Jewess, she did not like Judaism or its Scriptures (to put it mildly), but then she never knew them, she only thought she did – like many other assimilated anti-Jewish Jews of her class and time (French upper-middle moneyed and cultured class between the two world wars). I don't think she thought much of rabbis; in fact I doubt if she thought about them at all, and they repaid the 'compliment'.

So perhaps it is better that we never met officially; though perhaps we did meet unofficially quite often, since we both attended the little lunchtime concerts in London's National Gallery during the grey years after the fall of France in 1940. I sometimes wonder if she was the ruthless woman who slipped into the best placed seat before I could snatch it; or sometimes vice versa. While she was anorexically inclined, I was a neurotic, growing lad who stolidly munched disgusting war-time canary yellow cake (like cardboard smeared with artificial 'crème') right the way through Lieder, Quartets, Bach variations, and ravishingly delicate Debussy. I couldn't have been an aesthetic sight, but she must have looked a bit weird and war-worn too.

I must add in my own defence that lots of pious Christians, especially Catholics, are not very sure how to place her either, though Lord Longford thought she was the best spiritual thinker of his time. She probably believed an awesomely lot more of Catholic Christianity than they did and do, but she never fell into a font. Despite the fact that some very nice priests spent a lot of time over her, she exasperated all but the most patient.

To be fair, she had the same effect on Trotsky, who took shelter one night in her flat. He must have been tired out and she must have pelted him with sharp questions. He said it was the worst night in his life.

I liked her because she didn't waffle or evade the problems of her time and mine but dealt with them head-on: problems such as how God could have created such a nasty concentration camp and gulag-ridden world without being a super-sadist. I was suspicious when I first came across her essay on 'The Love of God and Affliction', but she didn't slide around the subject.

One thought of hers that I've been brooding over in the past few weeks is this: though we can never be certain if we are worshipping the true God, we can at least recognize and rid ourselves of the false ones. I think all of us 'religious folk' need to identify and name those false gods of ours. It's become urgent.

Why especially now? Because in the first part of the twentieth century it seemed that the secular ideologies, the secular religions if you like, were going to have it their own way. Lots of people believed in the coming enlightenment and were martyred for it. Two sweet, kind family friends, idealistic followers of the gentle Prince Kropotkin, actually returned to the Soviet Union to persuade Uncle Joe Stalin into the paths of liberty and decency. We never heard from them again.

I suppose Uncle Joe killed sixteen million plus and Hitler about the same, though more sadistically, and both were overtaken by the cultural revolutionists in China who may have murdered over twenty million. On a lesser scale, atheist countries like Albania were no-show places for the new Age of Reason.

After these atheist regimes exploded or imploded, only religion was left, and it made an unexpected comeback. Most war-exhausted, decent people were prepared to go along with it in some form or another, assuming it had learned from its past mistakes and corrected them.

But I'm afraid an awful lot haven't. They remain as un-reconstructed as ever. So here we go round the religious mulberry bush once again. The newspaper reports are dispiriting. In Russia some old-time believers seek to canonize Ivan the Terrible and Rasputin, which seems pretty sick to me. In Israel, some old-time rabbis want to reclaim Jewish 'rights' on the Temple Mount (why?), which would bury the peace process for ever. In Poland, I'm told, a pious radio station pours out old-time nationalism. Cocktails of piety and politics are still mixed by both sides in Northern Ireland. In Nigeria, a pregnant woman was condemned to death by stoning after giving birth because some say that's the price you pay for adultery in traditional religious law. In other new states, new freedom means imprisoning and executing gay minorities! Whew! And in many parts of Asia, places of one kind of worship are being torched or pulled down by devotees of another kind. Ancient Buddhas have been blasted out of their silent millenary existence. It is not a pretty picture.

Simone Weil was right – unfortunately. Before we jump to conclusions about the true God we hope we worship, let's identify the false ones we so often use as substitutes.

Now of course she would have said that it's no good just spotting other people's false gods – that's far too easy. We have to start with our own. So I've got to think hard about their presence in my own comfy 'enlightened' Judaism. I've started, and the probing is more disconcerting than I expected.

She was deeply suspicious of religion using short-cuts, such as worldly power, to gain other worldly aims. Religion wouldn't spiritualize politics – politics would just secularize religion.

I should have asked her about such things 70 years ago when we must have been sitting a few seats away from each other. It is the biggest 'might-have-been' of my life. What would she have thought, for example, of St Rasputin? It's something to brood over before I go to sleep.

Retreats

Where do you go and whom do you go to for further help on your spiritual progress? Do you need a teacher and, if so, how do you find one? The most obvious step is to enter the world of retreats. You can find lists of them on the internet or in religious bookshops.

There are a bewildering number and variety of them and somewhere in the lists there is certainly one that is right for you. There are Anglican, Roman Catholic and Free Church ones, Quaker ones, and occasional Jewish ones, including cabalist. There are Muslim ones too where you would be welcome – I have met non-Muslims who have attended Sufi or Dervish ones and been helped a lot. And the same goes for Buddhist ones: a friend of mine goes there to contemplate the end of his nose! There are now many more Buddhist monasteries (all schools and sects) than you might realize, especially since the exodus from Tibet. There are also ecumenical and New Age ones.

I enjoy reading through the lists. It's like opening a box of assorted spiritual chocolates with a different religious adventure in each. There are programmed, organized ones and, at others, you just melt into the resident community and become, for a weekend or week, a meek Quaker or a temporary nun, monk, friar, or Eastern ascetic.

What are they like? Their charges are moderate. They're not out to make money. If they're expensive and trendy and promise instant enlightenment I'd keep away; it doesn't fit the real thing.

On a retreat you can meditate or contemplate and at some Hindu ones even learn to levitate. (You have to be pretty advanced and supple for that.) At Evangelical ones you can speak in tongues (once again, something I've never done but I'm intrigued and ready to enjoy). You can also opt for total silence – which again is beyond me – like most Jews I enjoy words and chatter. You can paint and pray (together) – they make a good combination. You can study a super mystic at an Ignatian retreat (for advanced Christians) or break into the Interior Castle of Teresa of Ávila, or you can go simply to find yourself and something more. There's usually a user-friendly chapel with the presence of a Presence. I become very aware of it during the silence before I go to bed.

At a retreat you have company on your spiritual or religious journey. There are no single tables. The food is plain, to school dinners de luxe. Sometimes you even get a sherry before your school dinner. You sometimes help with the serving or washing-up. The latter is rather nice; the kitchen sink is a good place to get counselling from a teacher. Both of you are out of the rat-race, you can speak informally and personally, and you don't have to put on the style. If it's all strange and a bit alarming, many have soothing old-fashioned comforts, such as cocoa before bed, hot-water bottles and bars with other bottles. I've never encountered any which required me to sign up to any set beliefs, and nobody minds if you wander off to do your own thing.

If all of this sounds idyllic, I have to mention that I do find it unexpectedly hard to get going. Just as I am about to set off from home, I try to make excuses for not going. I tell myself that God is everywhere, so why do I have to traipse to the wilder parts of these islands to find him. (Answer: at home I'm too protected by my environment to let myself journey into another dimension.) Also, I'm a bit afraid. I'm not sure whether it's because something will happen or because nothing will happen.

Another oddity! The retreat houses which suited me best have been the decrepit ones. There was Dominican Spode (before it was sold off) which was built on a disused coal mine where the ground could open up in front of you, prompting thoughts of hell, as in Don Giovanni, and the Carmelite Boars Hill near Oxford before it became very comfy, cosy and chintzy where, in a deep freeze, I used to throw myself on board beds wrapped in my overcoat, not daring to take an icy shower but anointing myself with aftershave instead. In chapel I ponged something dreadful. I enjoyed helping in the kitchen there and wondered if I would like to be a monastery cook. These and other houses became my spiritual homes when I had problems – which was often. They welcomed me and it was nice to feel wanted. I learned a lot from the friars and novices. I was an only child and they became the brothers I never had and the nuns my sisters.

What did they give me?

They temporarily released me from the world and its worries (I've always suffered from anxiety states).

They pointed in the right direction – i.e. heavenwards. They understood the moments in my life when heaven happened to me and taught me how to integrate them.

They helped me stand aside from the rat-race outside me and inside me. I was very insecure.

They trusted me, though I didn't trust myself.

They became a substitute family and home. I was shattered when Spode was sold.

They understood the silence which spoke in the empty synagogue at my Confirmation.

Sometimes I met a patient, listening nun who was on my side.

The inner conversations continued in the long silences which followed the services.

I was never coerced, flattered or persuaded into any kind of conversion.

I must admit I never wanted to stay for a long time. I went often, but three days per visit was usually my limit. Being Jewish, I liked the worldly world too much – not for its riches but for the richness of its life. I liked busy markets and crowded charity shops, and Fred calling me to order in supermarket queues, and making love and munching cheap Danish caviar at parties, and meeting Fred during committees and in bars.

This is my story of retreats, but you must find your own way through this *embarras de richesses* and confusion. The one thing I am sure about is that there is something in them for you.

How do you find God Direct?

Dear Godseeker,

I enjoyed celebrating Passover for an old friend, Wendy (Dr Greengross), who'd come out of hospital, but what followed was as important to me as the rituals. My friend is a wise woman and a shrewd cookie, a retired GP, therapist and agony aunt. I envy her quick answers that only occur to me too late.

Someone exclaimed, 'What's the place of the Jewish mother?' 'In the wrong,' my friend retorted, 'Next question!' She tackles the problems most people avoid, like preparing bodies for burial according to the old pieties, writing a practical calendar of ageing, and concern for both the bodily and spiritual needs of the disabled. We clerics could learn a lot from the frankness of agony aunts.

'Did you enjoy Passover?' Wendy asked. Yes, I enjoyed her children's food, their acceptance of me and my partner as family, and her own deep feeling as she hallowed the candles. 'But I need something more than rituals,' I tell her, 'I need God Direct to teach me what kind of growing is growing old, and how to give up gracefully.'

'How do you find God Direct?' she asked, interested. After festivals are over I sit in a railway station, I tell her, if I can find a seat – smart shops are everywhere but free benches get fewer, and I watch the dramas of arrival and departure, people pushing and shoving like animals, and beggars staring longingly into boutique windows.

But then God directs my eyes to a porter soothing an angry man who's missed his train, and the forbearance of a queue as a young man wiggles his way to the front. God moves a tired Caribbean lady, noticing my stick, to insist on standing up, and then he moves into me and I'm moved to buy two sandwiches, one for me and one for whoever, and then I give up my seat to another grouchy oldie.

To my surprise, giving up makes me springy and hopeful again, and I sing aloud an old wartime song – 'Bless 'em all, bless 'em all, the long and the short and the tall . . .' – the porter, the angry man, my friend, the Caribbean lady and groucho especially. A bewildered foreign couple politely applaud, and I exit waving my stick like Maurice Chevalier; even groucho risks a grin.

I remember granny telling me about a rabbi in Poland who bumped into the spirit of the prophet Elijah at the local fair. 'Who is worthy of eternal life in this mob?' he asked, and Elijah pointed to some buskers. The puzzled rabbi went over to them and asked, 'What's your business here?' 'We make wives seem beautiful to their husbands and repair their quarrels with laughter.'

And I think I've got the answers to my problems!

Rabbi retreating solo into Nada (Nothing)

After the long liturgies of the Jewish High Holy days, my inner voice tells me it's time to retreat solo because we need to get together again privately. So I ring up the Discalced (no shoes) Carmelites at Boars Hill near Oxford and make arrangements. I'm busy, and they're busy, but they'll squeeze me in for two nights somehow. I can't risk him/it fading away on me. Like those worldly human friendships, my other-worldly one too requires time and attention. Who or what is my inner voice? It's the force inside me or outside me which leads me into self-honesty, kindness, generosity, and occasional flashes of transcendence. You can call it her/him/ Whomsover-Whatsoever/WW, your soul, your guardian angel, or Fred.

He's accompanied me through tricky times, and I use my imagination to reach him. Puzzling, but that's the truth, my truth. The proof of the pudding is in the eating.

I pack my bag and decide I don't want to go. Paddington is the most difficult station to get to, my partner will be alone, something dreadful will happen while I'm away, and Whomsover-Whatsoever (WW) can meet me just as well in my own kitchen. He can, but he doesn't, and it takes two to tango. I've gone through these hesitations so many times; they don't deter me. I'm too self-protected in the clutter of my own home, there's no room for anything to happen. Like my ancestor Abraham or John Bunyan, I have to go on an outer journey to make an inner one.

My friend drives me to Paddington. On the train I stoke up with railway fast comfort food, and a friar meets me at the other end. The house is quiet and I get smiles. I've been dropping in and out for about 30 years so they're family. I might become the oldest inhabitant. I'm given an older, less chintzy room, which reminds me pleasantly of the austerities of my first visit. There's a kettle nearby and a pack of chocolate-chip biscuits. How thoughtful!

I don't bother to unpack, but make for the chapel, where I sit in a corner at the back savouring the silence, which is full, not empty. I no longer screw my eyes up or make interesting things happen, I just enjoy the silence. I'm tired, so he can make the first move. I don't ask him to be present to me because he is. In his own time he'll show his hand.

There's a book lying around. I purloin it. It's a collection of extracts from John of the Cross, whom I find difficult. The English contemplatives are more homely like Julian of Norwich, honest dotty Margery Kempe, Bunyan, and Blake, etc.

I assume WW wants me to read the book. It's powerful stuff, but I don't like it. God has always come to me most clearly through witnessing the human tragedy and the human comedy, so what do I make of Nada – the Nothing of the world? But I do begin to understand the difference between meditation and contemplation. Another wave of affection! Perhaps he (WW) is laughing at me and my pretensions. In the empty chapel, I hum Sydney Carter's 'One more step' under my breath. That says it all for practical purposes.

I sit with the Fathers and Brothers at meals. As prayer makes me hungry and happy, I shine at small talk, and say funny things. They all hand me pots of this and that and the cook has provided a vegi treat. While washing up, a visitor asks me what I think of the Pope. I start to reply but then shut up. It's an honest question, but I'm not here for politics and personalities. They would derail me. Religious establishments don't enchant me, political ones don't either, nor some policies of Israeli governments. But the kindness of the Carmelites does.

As always, I have problems with the services – or rather with the books and texts. Some of it I can recite straightforwardly, some with my own curious glosses, while some are off my religious radar. The result is liturgical confetti, but no one seems to mind. They're a humble lot and no one is putting on the style – end of problem. They don't try to make windows into my soul. They let me make my own way to wherever.

In the afternoon, I actually sit in a field and consider the postcard scenery. I'm now more interested in the social life of the rabbits. I never was a nature boy except on boats. Dank green leaves and shivering sheep are a turn-off. I think about Nada/Nothing. It certainly gives me a fresh and awkward perspective on my life. I'll consult a down-to-earth Dominican friend. (Alas, he's dead, but I still talk to him.)

Before supper there's the long evening silence in which I think over my life with detachment but not Nada. I decide I like being an oldie and remind myself of the spiritual duties that go along with it, such as ending old quarrels, being truthful to myself, and not indulging in too easy 'solution-ism'. Before I go to sleep, I remember the liturgical lion 'who prowls around the priory to consume sinners'. I snore undisturbed.

It takes a day and more to adjust back to ordinary life. I'm rather silent, stuck between two realities.

N.B. Lots of retreat houses will try and fit you into their daily life. They might give you private chats (sometimes called 'conferences') if you ask politely. This is not analysis on the cheap!

The Holy Spirit in the steam

Dear Godseeker,

I'll be straight about my own credentials. I'm a gay, non-orthodox, establishment inclined, Jewish rabbi, who goes regularly to Christian retreat houses, and some of my best friends are nuns and friars. My C of E partner and I have been faithful for 27 years, though we're not legalized yet at a town hall because the Holy Spirit has already done it, otherwise we couldn't have made it together. We're OAPs with no children, just godchildren, which is enough, being more comfortable with our fellow oldies.

When some of the heat dies down, religions, gays and governments should try to come together – to talk *to* each other, not *at* each other; listening with more attention than they've shown in the past, and with enough humility to learn from each other and not be so dismissive – because, like the poor, churches and gays will always be with us. None can be wished away, however awkward.

I hope the following remarks about what religion can give to gays, and gays give to religion, may prove helpful. Being piggy in the middle (you must pardon the expression) is uncomfortable but instructive.

What can religion give gays? Some examples from experience:

The domestic ceremonies of my own religion help gays, excluded from their birth families, to create new families of friendship. They can also transform blank high-rise flats into homes. When partners hallow the Sabbath candles, blessing the bread and wine, they also hallow their life together. It's the real thing – you can feel it. Religion which helps straights stay together (though not that successfully) has been and is destructive with gay relationships. But gays can get the inner strength they need from God direct through prayer.

Religions can encourage gays to provide for their own oldies, sick and lonely, though, since the onset of HIV, this responsibility is already being learnt.

What can gays give religion? Some examples:

Many devoted clergy and religious who, because of their own experience of exclusion, work for all excluded.

Religion may be good about Higher Truth, but gays are better at honesty – about sex and sublimation in the spiritual life, for example.

They've got great resources of helpful humour, while establishment religion doesn't have nearly enough. Two Jewish women meet in the street. 'My son's a financial whizz-kid in the City,' says one. 'Mine's a homosexual,' says the other glumly. 'So where's his office?'

Such humour will be needed at the meetings I've proposed if there is courage enough to make them happen.

Unofficial seminary sauna in Amsterdam

Dear Godseeker,

Here are some intimate honest thoughts and experiences. 'The truth shall make you free' – even if it doesn't make you respectable.

At my official seminaries I quickly learned some unofficial lessons. They were these:

Religion tried for higher truth but it wasn't good at ordinary low honesty; to call a spade 'a bloody ——'. And to call my 'bits' something more specific than 'private parts', I had to visit Amsterdam Bohemia.

This was especially necessary because of the religious treatment (or non-treatment) of sex. I learned from it many truths about love but, for enlightenment about sex, I had to turn elsewhere. This problem was especially acute for me being a gay only child, whose parents had never got their act together.

I decided to finish with religion. But when I did, I got God Direct instead, to my surprise. They aren't the same, though they often overlap. In the sauna, I got to knew him as Fred, my Friend in high and low places. It seemed more suitable, more *comme il faut* in fact.

In a steamy kindly sauna I said yes to everything I had said no to for so many years. I went to it in desperation because my needs were influencing and falsifying my thinking and I was about to blow up from my own suppressed testosterone. I was honest with a priest, who recommended a monastery. The unreality of his advice shook me. I decided to leave England, and God with it, and crossed the North Sea.

In the sauna I had a religious experience and found that God had unexpectedly followed me, he had come with my luggage and was surprisingly vocal and practical, which the clerics I had met were not. After a mild orgy, rather like a sexual rugger scrum, I cried out in anger, 'Is this all it's about, a little light relief and that's it?'

The unexpected answer from on high or from within gobsmacked me. 'Lionel,' it said, 'you don't get much because you don't give much!' 'What are the rules for me here in a friendly permissive sauna for gay men of the older sort, just the ones I like?' I asked, 'What are the Ten Commandments of my new situation?' The following was revealed to me just before we were all politely served coffee and cake in the Dutch manner in our various stages of undress.

Don't do the night before what you're going to regret the morning after (very practical this because I was the worrying type).

If you make an appointment to meet someone, keep it, even if you've met someone more attractive between times.

If the person you're going to say no to is an oldie, be especially considerate. Remember, if you're lucky you might become an oldie too!

Don't flee like a scalded cat from someone you've just made love to. It's demeaning for the other person as well as for you. Love and sex need good manners and affection – not rejection.

Don't hand out blank cheques on the affections you can't cash or dates for meetings you won't keep. In Bohemia, the difference between heaven and hell is trust. It's fragile. Keep it!

Did I keep them all from that moment on? No, but they were my compass and, over time, I have assimilated them. God had spoken. I had called to the Lord, and Fred had answered me. God be thanked. I had got what my official seminaries couldn't give me.

In return I tried to see my fellow clients as my Friend Fred saw them, not in the formal canon law categories I'd learned in seminars, but as they really were. For example, if procreation is not present, which is the situation for most gays and many straights, what is left? A great deal more than a tumble in the hay! People sleep with each other (a curious term) and make love because they are lonely or tense; it is a way to make contact with another human being, to escape the confines of the ego, to give pleasure and to receive it. It is a way to relax and go to sleep and to attend to the body's needs. It is a way to give comfort and pleasure and warmth. It can be 'fun', which is a difficult and unusual concept in religion. There isn't much in any of our Scriptures. In them Fred is angry or agonized. He is righteous or wrathful, he frowns, judges and favours. He rarely laughs and never winks, unless perhaps you can read that into the text at the end of the book of Jonah.

In homosexual relations the situation is even more chaotic. Traditional religious systems have typed people by their outer genitalia, not by their inner feeling. In this, unrefined religion and hard porn have much in common. Neither does people justice. So the form of a relationship, rather than its content or depth, has been made the object of concentration.

But now I saw the reality with the new sight and insight I had learned under the benevolent gaze of Fred.

In the sauna, I re-learned something I'd always known but never recognized: that some marriages are made in heaven and some are only made for money. Some deserve the name; with others it is only a name. Some progress from 'in love' to love itself and the commitment that comes with it. Some are permanent in form but temporary in nature. Some are for mutual convenience, without love. In some the bond is hostility; and the marriage is little more than a licence to destroy each other. The same phenomena apply to unmarried relationships and partnerships as well. These days the form tells you less and less as to which is which. Forms are easier to administrate than content, so all institutions, whether religious or secular, concentrate on them.

In the naked sauna, Fred also showed me the naked truth. Like Dante's Virgil, he showed me heaven and hell. A bitter oldie who frightened me and whose brutal advances I rejected politely, spread a rumour around that I had a terrible disease, which I didn't, and that everybody should keep away from me. Fortunately I had learned from the straightforwardness of the Dutch and politely but firmly explained the situation. What a relief! That was a taste of hell. I also met a young handsome Frenchman who chatted up the oldest oldie ruins there. There's no accounting for tastes, I thought and, Dutch style, asked him about his rather unusual preferences. They weren't his preferences he told me, but someone ought to look after their needs too, which he did. That was heaven. It was quite simple.

Hell is where people hate and hurt each other. Heaven is where they help each other.

Once again, seeing things through Fred's eyes in the sauna also taught me the limits of my own goodness, the hard way. I enjoyed myself a lot there and made some very good friends, but I also learned the limits of my friendship. I met one lovely chap who had a terminal illness. He thought when he met me that a messiah had come into his life and I issued a cheque of affection I couldn't cash. I had played at being an angel and this was a destructive fantasy because I was no angel – or only in sermons.

Before I left Holland I learned another very important lesson. The kind lady who managed the sauna had cancer. I visited her in hospital. Some time later I was told that she had died and her funeral would take place in a few days' time, just before I would be delivering a lecture on religious experience. I decided not to go because I couldn't risk a scandal. In any case, I comforted myself, I would not be missed as so many other people would come to pay their respects. But I learned later that hardly anyone had turned up to accompany her on her last journey. They must have shared my problem, for she had many professional clients, some clergy like me. I felt a real heel, and Fred didn't deny it. In fact he told me unless I put my life to rights we wouldn't be seeing each other much more. Someone also told me that she had been married to a Jew and she had stood by him throughout the Nazi occupation.

I told Fred not to worry. When I got back to England, I would 'come out'. 'About time, dearie,' he said, 'about time – you nearly lost your soul over that one!'

God bless

I noticed a Dominican church by my holiday hotel so I went in to remember my Dominican friend Father Gordian who'd just died and whose funeral I'd missed because it was my turn at the hospital. Old friends dying on you gets more frequent as you get older, but our friendship of 40 years was irreplaceable; even the rows. He was the big brother I never had who eased my worries to get to sleep.

There's been so much overheated strident religion lately. Gordian's God-given common sense always took me by surprise. 'How do you ease your problems?' I'd asked. He talked to cows, he said, who gathered round him. They couldn't understand but were muzzily sympathetic. 'Try it,' he said; and it worked.

My God, I'd miss him. But you don't have to miss him, whispered an inner voice. People you've loved carry on living in you, if you give them mind room. Which I did, and there he was, in my imagination as it were. 'How's things, Gordian?' I said curiously. 'What's your problem, Lionel?' he said, coming straight to the point. Eternity hadn't changed him, and I eagerly recited my latest woe. 'Give it to God, Lionel,' he said tersely. 'That's what he's there for. It's not your sort of problem – write your book instead.' I took the advice and had a happier holiday and began this book!

I once asked him what original sin meant. 'Knowing this world's imperfect, and you are too, and acting accordingly.' What a relief! I didn't have to feel guilty because I didn't have perfect answers to the problems in this morning's news: whether it is 1914-type Balkan hatreds – play it again Sam! – or how to prop up Afghanistan, or exporting democracy to countries which can't work it out or don't want it.

Which doesn't stop me offering my place at the check-out to a harassed mum, or my seat on the bus to someone older than I am, if such exists, for the small good deeds I do lead to bigger ones beyond me, as taught by those practical rabbis whom Gordian admired.

Or what about cheering you up in these troubled times, dear readers, with one of Gordian's stories of commonsense saints (though he thought this one was apocryphal).

St Teresa of Ávila was travelling with her nuns at night in a closed wagon which skidded, depositing the nuns in a ditch. 'Pray for us, Mother Teresa,' they cried. So Teresa knelt in the ditch and prayed. 'Lord,' she said tartly, 'since this is how you treat your friends, it's no wonder you have so few of them!' If I'd been a sixteenth-century Mother Superior in a Spanish ditch at night, I'd have said the same, if I'd had the Chutzpah, of course.

Thanks, Father Gordian, I'll always bear you in mind.

I'll also bear you in mind, as will my partner, because you were one of the very few who really believed in our unlikely relationship. Thank you for offering to journey across England to explain us to each other. That's real friendship.

Chapter 8

Hospitalization

Introduction

As you get older, hospitals become a way of life; especially now, when every year our lives are extended whether we want it or not. At present, I do want it – at least up to the point of unnecessary pain. Hospitals are turning out to be the best seminaries I've ever attended. We learn a lot; sometimes a bit too much for comfort.

A degree in kindness

I sit in the hospital waiting-room, well named for there's indeed a lot of waiting. But I've no complaints; I've packed a bag of smoked salmon-bit sandwiches, a kitchen roll, a work book, a novel with a reliably happy ending, and diet cola. And during blood tests I think of what I'll make for supper tonight. I like people-watching. For an octogenarian, hospital waiting becomes almost a way of life. While munching my salmon bits, I ponder a piece of news I almost missed: nurses will get three-year degrees, not just two-year diplomas. I'm glad for them and for me, for the technology of medicine gets more complex monthly.

But it's kindness from nurses which has helped me as much as technology, and I hope that that doesn't get lost in the system. I don't forget words like, 'Well, me poor darlin', let's see if we can get yer going today – yer's a brave lad.' I thank her profusely and she remarks to the ward, 'Well, it can't be me beauty so it must be me charm', and pirouettes away with my dirty laundry – setting me up for the day.

And I think of the nurse who popped a teddy bear into a young man's bed to await his return from a hard time in the treatment room.

And then after my electronic treatment, I startled the nurses by complaining that the monster machine was squeaking. 'But it cost millions,' they protested. Helpfully I recommend a can of WD40 or Three-In-One oil from the garage. Later on, I discover that a caring nurse had recorded a tape of bird song to calm us anxious patients – and that's the squeaking. We laugh – but God bless her.

In an oldies ward, my neighbour grunts and gurgles, cuddling his pillow. Nurse passes by. Closing his curtain, she whispers, 'I'll bring tea and clean you up in fifteen minutes.' 'His wife died a few weeks back,' she whispers to me, 'and he misses her that bad – do you have a text to help him?' I whisper back a tombstone inscription from a man to his wife: 'Tonight I sleep alone, but one morning we shall wake together.'

So the problem is, 'How do you teach kindness?' – especially if you haven't experienced much as a child. Perhaps by remembering the kindnesses you've received and the unkindnesses you've suffered and what both felt like, and also the kindnesses you've shown and the unkindnesses you've inflicted, and how you catch kindness from people, like measles, not from books. A lot of unkindness comes because people don't like themselves. So, take credit for the good you've done, treat yourself kindly and you'll be kinder to others.

The old rabbis said the Temple was destroyed not by Roman might but because people weren't kind or generous enough to each other – if our world goes bust, it will be for the same reason.

Click, click in hospital

I meditate on my own exhaustion. I'd forgotten I was no longer a
sprightly 70 but 80 and coming to bits. So I lose my balance, tumble
down stairs, and crash into a cupboard. My partner, though an ath-
letic 84, can't raise my fourteen stone so rushes outside and returns
with an ambulance.

Then our multiethnic and much under-appreciated NHS swings
into action because I've got a soaring temperature. And I doze, com-
fortably secured by a drip, ear-plugged to my transistor, and half-
listening to the familiar news. There are the reformers who can't
reform themselves, terrorists covering their own inner violence
under a fig-leaf of faith, spiritual teachers for instant drugged
enlightenment, and our old acquaintances the charismatic revolu-
tionaries shouting 'Power to the people' – but the corruption
remains. We fool ourselves, like the people between the two world
wars.

But then my godly inner voice whispers, 'It's too easy, Lionel,
exposing other people's hypocrisies; what about your own ego
games, your hidden agendas and mixed motives? Where's your self-
honesty?'

'But I'm sick and growing old,' I answer querulously. 'But you're
not dead yet,' says my inner voice brightly. 'Whether you're growing
up, growing fat or growing old, you're still growing.'

Eighty is a good age to be honest to God and to make a new start
in life. But this kind of knowledge doesn't come easy, and you'll need
courage from prayer to face it and humour to puncture your false
pride. We humans are too tricky-clever to be wise, which might
prove our undoing. Broad indeed is the way which leads to self-
deception and cloud cuckoo-land.

A man marches into a wine bar. 'Seven glasses of bubbly,' he
orders – and drinks them one by one. The following week he does

the same. The curious waiter asks him why. 'I used to come here with my six brothers and sisters, and we each had a glass to celebrate the weekend. But now I'm the only one left hereabouts and this is how I remember our happy family.'

'Thanks for telling me,' said the waiter, much moved. So he's shocked when the man returns a week later and asks for only six glasses of bubbly. 'Has anything happened to one of your brothers or sisters?' he asks fearfully. 'Oh no,' said the man. 'They're doing fine. I've just stopped drinking, that's all.'

Mrs Cohen takes her son Issy to see the psychiatrist. After Mrs Cohen leaves them, the psychiatrist examines Issy and then calls her back.

'Well, Mrs Cohen,' he says kindly. 'There is nothing really wrong with your Issy, except that he has a slightly over-developed Oedipus complex.'

'Oh, doctor, doctor,' she says happily. 'Oedipus, Shmoedipus, what do I care, so long as he loves his mummy!'

O Lord, help us to have mercy on ourselves, then we might show more mercy to others for, as you know, we're more mad than bad (and whose fault is that?).

The spirituality of the NHS

Dear Godseeker,

As I have said, hospitals continued my spiritual education long after my seminary education stopped. And, no, I don't mean chaplains' visits and service times in hospital chapels, but something more personal.

Hazily I remember coming out of an anaesthetic blessing the NHS because, without it, I'd have been a gonner long ago. I know the problems – your file's lost, your call's cut off, your treatment's on/off/on or you've met a bug or a bully. But I can also remember life before the existence and help of the NHS.

You could see a doctor for a shilling – but who had a shilling? If you touched bottom there was either the Sally Army or the Medical Mission to the Jews. I don't remember reciting Christian prayers, but my maternal granny still washed my mouth out in case I had been blasphemous.

Also professional thanks for my spiritual lessons from the NHS and hospices. At my seminary I learned religion from books but in wards I learned spirituality from experience. Coming to on my trolley, I mentally clicked those hospital friends as Arab friends click their worry beads – as remembrancers.

Click: However bad you are, in a ward there is always someone worse off than you are, so you can concentrate on others and don't drown in self-pity.

Click: My teachers in spirituality were ordinary patients. A newcomer is wheeled into the ward, bellicose yet scared. He's in denial and threatening to sue everybody and give God a black eye. Other patients eased him into crying and acceptance and, incidentally, taught me compassion.

Click: The NHS is concerned with the whole you, not just your bumps and lumps. A social worker was worried about my pets and who was feeding them and who would welcome me home with a cuppa. She taught me congregational care.

Click: In a small hospice, consultants, cleaners, nurses and patients lunched around the kitchen table serving each other. Sickness didn't mean separation but becoming a family, a holy family, though religion wasn't mentioned.

The current debates on the NHS understandably centre on budgets and bureaucracy. The heart of the NHS is damaged, but it is still concerned with hurt, worried folk who can get lost amid the politics and pressures.

So a click to the medics at Christmas, dressed up as surreal bunnies; though I nearly died laughing.

And another to those who feel for the very few dying patients in unbearable pain which even palliative care can't yet control who want to regulate their own dying, accepting all safeguards. Whether I'd regulate my own dying I don't know, because God has sometimes come closest when I'm at my lowest and I don't like to miss out. But that should be my decision.

At a conference on spirituality, I was proud of our country: in the immediate post-war years we had been pioneers of compassionate living and dying.

Chapter 9

Scriptures of Tradition and Personal Scriptures of Life Experience

Introduction

Why this conflict in the nature of things, this eternal struggle between truth and truth? (Boëthius)

Not between truth and lies, but between truth and truth!

And this, dear Godseeker, can be the unexpected consequence of your own religious experience: tradition and religion say one thing – and God, Fred and your conscience may say another. Which is why institutional religion is wary of your own 'this life and beyond' experience. The fear of such a contradiction can be so fearful that Godseekers have even burned each other at the stake.

Having had the same problem with Marxism, I decided I would make an accommodation and live tactfully with the conflict, finding it both stimulating and enlightening. But I was always a free-range type rather than a battery believer and, on the whole, provided the 'class' seems right, eccentrics are permitted in the UK, even well treated.

One kind of authority is outside of us and another within us. There is the scripture of 'them, then' and the scripture of 'me, now'. Yes, I 'pick 'n' choose', and don't try to believe the lot, because a lot of tradition is unbelievable, at least in the way it is presented, and so is a lot of one's own subjective experience. But you are responsible for your own accommodation. Over to you!

Private prayers

It could be my mother's mother's anniversary, the one who brought me up – 'could be' because her papers and pieces got blown up during the Blitz, along with the kitchen she lived in and the cemetery they buried her in. All I have left of her is one plate, a photograph tinted to look like an oil painting, and the cooking and kindness I learned from her as she fed neighbours on the dole, the mad woman down the street, her beggars, and striking Welsh miners, as well as me – and all this on pennies. I went down to old Jewish East London to pay my respects, but even the street we lived in was gone – a land-mine had flattened it and the council built flats on it that covered all memories.

I didn't go just because of piety; I wanted to work out the scripture of my own life whose horizon was coming ever nearer, and I needed to know what I really believed, if I believed at all. I couldn't lean on illusions.

Granny would have turned to the traditional Scriptures, the ones with a capital 'S', and why didn't I do the same? Because they're a puzzle. They're about 'them, then' people long ago and far away, and I was interested in 'me, now'. So how do we relate, and are those Scriptures true? They're a mixture of what happened, what people wanted to have happened, and the meaning of what happened – and I can't separate them. Also the miracles, which encouraged the faith of granny who was medieval, put me off because I'm a modern like my ma. Applying ancient laws and customs to modern conditions brings disaster. The awful results festoon the pages of our newspapers: ancient creeds contain both junk and treasure.

For granny, those scriptures of tradition were the centre of her life, and her life was a commentary around them. For me it's the reverse, and I think this is so for many of you too.

In a democratic age, revelation comes to us democratically. If we put together honestly the little bits of truth we've learned in life – like pieces in a jigsaw – then God's face or message will emerge from it.

These are some of my 'little bits' – none of them are original:

- 'Your successes will make you clever, but only your problems will make you wise.'
- 'We need a religious home – not a religious prison.'
- 'Love people as they are, not as you want them to be.'
- 'Religion is the art of giving without strings.'
- 'I have seen the nature of good and know that it is beautiful. I have seen the nature of evil and know that it is ugly.'
- 'If you trust and lean on nothing, that nothing will support you.'

And now a Yiddish joke which reminds me of my granny who loved me as I was.

A Jewish gangster from East London piously visits his mother every Sabbath evening. As he knocks at her door, a rival gang who were lying in wait for him shoot him down and, as she opens the door, he slithers down, bleeding. 'They've got me, ma,' he whispers. 'Soup first, darling, we can talk later,' she says firmly. That was my gran!

Late arrival at traditional Scriptures

Dear Godseeker,

I came to God inside me by myself, and a love affair fairly quickly ensued, as I've already described. This was to be expected because it is not difficult to make God in one's own image and to fall in love with your reflection. But I was no fool and aware of the danger, and I did not intend to end up in a nuthouse or psychiatric ward, most of which have a quota of believers who believe too much too easily. I was rescued from that lapse by undergoing a rigorous radical Freudian analysis at the same time as my hesitant conversion. In fact it was only my inner religion which made me able to stand up to the rigours of that analysis to its bittersweet end. So, though my analysis left me confused, it helped me to trust my inner experience rather than denying its validity.

I did not come to the traditional Scriptures of religion until much later. Even as a child I was aware of the holes in the arguments for them. The East End of London was multireligious and multiethnic long before the rest of the country caught up because it was by the London docks where new immigrants disembarked. So at school my fellow classmates were Irish Catties, C of E, Six County Protties, Sally and Church Armies, assorted commies split between the Third and the Fourth Internationals which function like religions, some Hindus and Muslims, and a lot who would be anything which handed out food parcels and coach awaydays to Southend. The last were the most rational. There must have also been some Black and Brown Shirts, but they didn't show themselves in my street or school – wisely, as about one-third of the pupils were Jewish. I still admire our teachers who tried to be fair to this ideological zoo.

One problem was obvious; each denomination believed it was right and the others fatally flawed or, at best, charitably misguided. We relayed to each other in the playground what parents had told us to say or shout if an argument broke out and push turned to shove – as it frequently did. But it was also obvious that they couldn't all be right, including flawed Yids like my own lot. Miracles were adduced in support of the religious positions. I didn't and don't take kindly to them. They don't help but hinder my belief – well, that is how it is for me. By miracles I don't mean rationalized pasteurized ones but the full-blooded holy showbusiness kind. The only person I really trusted was my cynical revolutionary grandpa who still kept to kosher food for health reasons.

'Lionel,' he said, 'if you live like a good Jew in this life, God might reward you by letting you live like a goy (a non-Jew) in the next.' (I think he meant ham and jellied eels.) This seemed only fair to me, but it didn't convert me back to the ways of my fathers. Nor did my evacuation nor my Confirmation, both of which I have already described. I was also observant about the realities – one of which was that my adults would pay hard-earned money to get a teacher to get me to believe what they themselves didn't or couldn't believe.

Later on, as I got to know more history, I couldn't see the point of inflicting the morals and manners of the Bronze Age onto the present generation. So much for the legal system in the Old Testament. I didn't trust the miracle-stuffed New Testament either. They were all embedded in their time and fit for a museum – apart from a sentence or two or three here and there which made me pause. They all claimed too much, and the more they claimed, the less I trusted them – all of them – irrespective of race, religion or creed.

It was commonsense reasonable biblical criticism which sort of restored the Scriptures to me. I tried to read them through after I was evacuated. As semi-historical documents they were fascinating but bizarre. But there was so much bad temper, and elitism, and extremism in them – they couldn't provide a ways of life for me. But what wonderful love stories! Like Naomi & Ruth and David & Jonathan (both same-sex stories – make of that what you will!).

Then I began to study the books of the Bible with teachers at my seminary who really loved them. Dr Ellen Littman, a refugee from Berlin, taught me Jonah. It was the first biblical book I had ever studied. It wasn't just a cartoon story of a prophet living in a whale, but the holy of holies in the biblical library and the most courageous self-criticism a people had ever canonized about itself. And, as I have said, there were sentences and books which amazed me by their breadth. Dr Littman told me how a Nazi teacher had tried to justify the Nazi racial laws to her by citing Ezra and his order to put away foreign, non-Jewish, wives. But she trumped the teacher by saying, 'But we also have a book of Ruth. Where is yours?'

If the Bible is an argument not a conclusion, I can go along with it and take part in it. If it is only the latter, then it is no longer a living book but an embalmed relic and, as such, possibly dangerous. Honouring it is not kissing it or processing it, but developing it, correcting it with our later knowledge, and probing its truth in our life experience. I had made the join!

So late in life I have recovered my own Jewish Scripture and lots of bits of other Scriptures too. My granny would have been pleased. But there will always be a difference between the way she regarded them and the way I do. I can illustrate this difference by a diagram. In Jewish tradition, the biblical books are printed in the centre of the page and are then surrounded by circles of printed commentaries of later times. The effect is rather like a cross-section of a tree and very decorative. For granny, the holy text was the central Scripture and her life was another tiny commentary around it. For me it is the opposite: my own life experience is the centre and the Scriptures are the commentary on that. Perhaps my attitude will change as I get closer to life's horizon, but I don't think so.

Many modern people do not like to admit this. They adhere to what I call the two-drawer system. In this the ritual and religious life is in a separate drawer away from the tensions of modern street life, and the two do not relate or, if they do, only by the use of paradox. I can understand this, but cannot accept it for myself. Such consolations of religion are denied me – thank God!

Dear Godseeker, I do not know whether this personal outpouring is helpful to you. But I had to make it to explain myself as I am now. Fortunately we are on a journey. We know, or think we know, what we are but we do not know what or where we shall be. A scientist said that the cosmos we live in is not merely stranger than we think but stranger than we could ever think – and his words give us pause.

I repeat the test I have given before. If your beliefs make you kinder and more generous and more honest to yourself about yourself, you're on the right road whatever anyone else says. Go for it!

For reading on the road, I have found the following books helpful – I read them randomly and not necessarily from beginning to end:

* William James (brother of Henry), *The Varieties of Religious Experience.*
* Joseph Campbell, *The Hero with a Thousand Faces.*
* Rudolf Otto, *The Idea of the Holy.*
* Jonathan Magonet, *A Rabbi's Bible.*

And these books will lead to others.

If it all gets too much for you, then I suggest any anthology of Jewish humour as profound, broad and vulgar as you like, to join you, your soul and Fred, and the Eternal, and WW together in a good laugh.

There are not enough jokes in Scriptures (with the exception of Zen). Perhaps you can write some in the margins around those sacred texts with their so serious commentaries.

The ram's horn – making sense of a tradition

Perhaps you can blow a ram's horn, but I can't. Unlike my colleagues, I can't coax the tiniest note out of it, just a mouthful of spittle. If you whistle, I'm told you get a good trumpet blast of biblical sound – but I can't whistle either.

But blowing the ram's horn is important ritually because it recalls a biblical time about 4,000 years ago when, instead of sacrificing his son, Isaac, Abraham sacrificed a ram caught in a thicket, and the blast from the ram's horn reminds us even now of Abraham's devotion. More practically today it's blown at the Jewish New Year service as a warning siren, rather like the air-raid sirens some of us remember from the Second World War, which told us enemy planes were approaching and we should take shelter fast.

But in the Jewish New Year and the Day of Atonement services, the ram's horn doesn't warn us about bombs but about our sins which are also too close for comfort and which can do untold damage unless we defuse them in time.

In the synagogue, here's what that wailing sound alerts me to:

·   Promises I haven't kept.
·   Letting old quarrels hang around long after their sell-by date; after you and the other person have long forgotten what the quarrel was all about. A phone call might do the trick or an invitation to tea or even a Jewish New Year card. That should startle them, especially if they are not Jewish. You may risk rejection from them – but not from God.
·   Bearing grudges – the ram's horn says if there's trouble at home, talk it out. The houses I loathed visiting as a minister were those where the couple sat in frozen silence at opposite ends of the room, only talking at each other through me.
·   A wise colleague of mine said we all change and our needs change with us, and in a good marriage the couple divorce and remarry many times, always re-finding each other on a deeper level. Having rows is only human, but making up can be divine – especially when accompanied by colcannon (Irish mashed potatoes), smoked salmon and Irish coffee.

- The Jewish New Year is a festival which commemorates no worldly victory or defeat. We remember instead the teachings of the prophets, 'Hath not one father created us, so aren't we family to each other?'

These are the thoughts the ram's horn awakes in me. It's a spiritual tonic, though I still agree with the Jewish comedian Danny Kaye that musically 'It's an ill wind that no one blows good!'

Also a Jewish folk saying – 'Love is nice, but it's nicer with herrings!'

The Scripture of your own life

My friend, Annelies, insisted on living on her own even in old age. 'I am one of those people who are content with their own company,' she said. And I admired her because I've never reached that blessed state. In her nineties she was immobilized and I asked her what she did all day. 'I think about my life,' she said. 'Even now it's not too late. I still have to learn the lessons embedded in it.'

She certainly had a lot of life to ponder. She was born into a secure cultured Berlin family, but grew up in the barbarian Nazi time. When her husband was arrested by the Gestapo, she hurriedly fled with her baby daughter and finally joined him interned on the Isle of Man. Later on, she had to find her feet in a new country with a new language.

I understood what she was telling me. She was a rabbi's wife who had listened to many Scriptures, but all these had to be supplemented and sealed by her own personal private scripture which she had to work out for herself.

As a youngster I wasn't interested in personal private scriptures that I had to work out myself. I didn't want complexity; it was too much like hard work. I wanted simplicity. I wanted instant truth and guaranteed ideologies which relieved me of having to think for myself, and for which I didn't have to take responsibility. I wanted people who had all the answers.

So I shouted slogans in Marxist processions and sang hymns to uncritical nationalisms, enjoyed showbiz religions which knew exactly what God had for breakfast, and ideologies and theologies which had all the answers. I only deserted them reluctantly after I got my first hundred wrong answers!

Because of my own life experience, I understand very well the attraction of totalitarian ideologies and religious reach-me-downs.

Private practical honest prayer!

For many, prayer is not turning over pages in a liturgy or chanting words, but a relationship, a friendship, or a love affair which follows its own course as the relationship deepens and the presence of God or heaven becomes more and more real in day-to-day life – a continuing inner conversation.

These are some of the words I use. I've set them down as an example and encouragement for those whose prayer life takes this simple, basic conversational form. They may seem banal (they are), but the language of love sounds like that if you are an outsider, not a participant.

- **For frequent and general use:** 'Help!'
- **Considering old age:** 'It's not a pretty prospect. But problems can turn into opportunities. I've seen it happen. Give me courage and I'll try to give you the benefit of the doubt!'
- **Compassion for God:** 'The world you created is an awful mess and you must take your share of the blame. I'm sorry for you, because I think you blundered but meant well. I'll try to help you clean it up – repair it.'

- **Before going on in a theatre – or in a pulpit:** 'Dear Fred – stick around – so I'm not trapped by my own ego games.'
- **Chairing a meeting:** I put Fred in an empty chair, which firms up his presence and stops my own fantasies of power.
- **Gratitude:** 'Thank you for making heaven happen. I've seen some generous things today, which lit me up like Sabbath candles.'
- **Death:** 'I'm tired and I'd like to go home. Perhaps you'll recycle me!'
- **Morning/evening prayers mean singing:** 'One more step . . .' by my old friend Sydney Carter. I sing it in the shower or on the way to work. At night I commune with others. I sing 'Bless 'em all, bless 'em all', i.e. bless everybody – and try to mean it.

If you start from where you are in life and what you're thinking, you can be surprised by what your silly self-centred prayer can turn into. Start by telling God what's really worrying you – aloud!

Which Scripture?

There are two confusions which I can't sort out for you because I haven't sorted them out in myself. The first relates to the names I give to God which have changed and evolved throughout my lifetime and which are discussed in detail earlier in this handbook.

The second concerns Scripture.

As I've said, my approach to Scripture is a bit messy. But then the greatest Scriptures are a bit messy too. There are bits of about half-a-dozen creation stories in the Hebrew Scriptures (i.e. The Old Testament) and none are the same. The first account, in Genesis 1 v. 1, starts: 'In the beginning . . .' and, in Genesis 2 v. 4 there is a different creation story which begins, 'These are the generations . . .'

These two accounts of creation just lie side by side, different in purpose, in their sophistication or lack of it, and in their imagery and provenance.

There are two versions of the Ten Commandments too: one in Exodus and one in Deuteronomy, once again fulfilling different purposes. The same events are reported differently in the book of Kings and the book of Chronicles – their writers, whoever they were, had different political axes to grind. There is also the commonsense wisdom of Proverbs and the life experience of Ecclesiastes which contradicts it.

Similarly, in the Gospels, the different books don't fit together seamlessly. Some leave out the birth stories, or give Jesus different genealogies or family details. Once again, the result is a creative mess, creative because in Scripture, as well as in clothes, one size doesn't fit all, and we come to such books or rather 'libraries of books' with different needs and preoccupations, speaking to us over centuries.

I wish to point out one difference which is important in my life and interpretation which does not cover centuries but just the time which elapsed between my granny's death before the Second World War and my own growing awareness at infant school of the problem of Boëthius (I'd never heard of him then) about the clash in the nature of things, not between truth and lies, but between truth and truth.

To my grandparents (may their memory be for a blessing!), Scripture was the traditional Hebrew Text surrounded by circles of later rabbinic commentary: and they saw their lives as just another slender commentary on that basic Holy Text.

I do not see things like that and never shall because in between me and my grandparents has come the Enlightenment, a scientific revolution, biblical criticism (higher and lower), an English education and an accompanying secular revolution in society.

For me that old received text has one great limitation – it was compiled long ago and far away. It was about 'them then', not about 'me now'. So for me, text and commentary have changed places. My basic text is my own life experience and the old received text is now a commentary on that. And that is why my direct experience of God or Whomsoever-Whatsoever is so important to me and probably to you also, and our experiences are really the subject of this book. I do not think we can read the traditional Scriptures without affixing to them the scriptures (with a small 's') of our own lives. Those small scriptures are the connecting link between past and present. They enable the great Scriptures of tradition to speak.

If you want a more certain external authority, there is none. Even if you are fundamentalist, you choose your own brand of fundamentalism and which Scripture or religion you are fundamentalist about, and there are many available. You have to take responsibility for what you believe. You become what you believe – you become your own truth – so be careful, it can be dangerous!

I remember from many decades ago a cartoon of Steig of *New Yorker* fame. In it you see a man holding himself up in mid-air by his own hand underneath his feet. He is speaking to you. 'Who am I', he asks smugly, 'to have an opinion of my own?'

Heresy in the Holy Book – what a relief!

Dear Godseeker,

The Bible can surprise even pious folk like us. It certainly surprised me just when I was trying to be God's good boy; not just pious but over-pious or 'pi'. After the book of Jonah, I leafed through some pages and found Ecclesiastes – which I suppose means 'The Committee-Men' in today's English usage. Take chapter 7 verse 6 for example: the words are simple but hardly pious. 'Don't be righteous overmuch', it says, which can mean don't be over-righteous or too righteous or hit someone over the head with your righteousness, as my grandma used to mutter caustically in Yiddish, or hide your aggression under some righteous slogans as rioters often do, or be self-righteous and overdo it.

Now you might mutter, equally caustically, that I would say that, wouldn't I? And I accept your criticism because my life, like yours, has its unrighteous patches.

Like most human beings, I'm not cut out for instant sanctity. I fall down in life, pick myself up, fall down again, and pick myself up again. Repentance for me doesn't mean wringing my hands but learning a bit more about my soul and the world every time I fall down so that in the end I learn not to fall down again – at least not in the same way.

I want to be righteous and clean but not over-righteous and squeaky clean because that way you fall into another lot of sins such as false pride, hard-heartedness or hypocrisy. Over-righteous people are tempted to gloat over other people's falls from grace – a very creepy sin indeed.

It's difficult sorting out morality from moralism, piety from just being pi, and righteousness from self-righteousness. Here are some sayings I learned from my teachers which helped me spot real religion, and I pass them on.

- Guide yourself by the stars, but don't think you'll land on them.
- A righteous person looks after his own soul and other people's bodies. A hypocrite looks after his own body and other people's souls.
- Beware of perfectionism – just try to do a little bit better each day. Start off with small things like stopping politely to tell someone the time or not pushing in a queue. Such small things will get you into the habit of goodness. And that's the surest way to heaven.

- It's very tempting to try a short-cut and force other people into righteousness – your own sort, of course. There was Cromwell's Government of Saints which ended in dictatorship, and Prohibition in America which resulted in a government of gangsters. Many religious groups are trying it now all over the world. The results are repressive and even horrific.
- Take the advice of the Bible – 'be righteous but not overmuch'!
- Be warned by this over-zealous minister who had to sit in a crowded train next to a drunk. 'What's gout?' the drunk suddenly shouted. The minister saw his chance for a quick conversion. 'Gout', he said impressively, 'is a disease brought on by booze, gluttony and sex.' 'Well,' said the drunk, 'it says here that the bishop's got it.'

Your own scripture – buy yourself a notebook!

You will need your own scripture to unlock the traditional Scriptures, a new scripture about 'me now'. How do you go about writing the scripture of your own life?

Well, first of all, you don't have to write it down unless you want to. You need only think it, compose it and ponder it, unless of course you want to publish it like I do. Some Godseekers will only share it with God, because it is too intimate for anyone else. Some will share it with those they love. But, like my mother, I am garrulous and have no shame.

Your own book, whether published or not, is mentioned in the liturgy for the holiest days of the Jewish year which talks about the Book of Life, the book that records your life – which is signed with your life.

So I suggest you buy yourself a notebook and record in it what has touched your soul, and what perceptions you have had of the life of the world beyond, of another dimension.

You could also use prayer beads or a rosary or tied knots (Jewish style) as remembrancers. These are devices of great antiquity for Godseekers.

Your book is unique, and the test is not its form or aesthetics but the combination of humble honesty with higher truths.

These are the stages I've gone through while Godsearching or Godhunting. They aren't top quality experiences but they're what happened to me.

I went into religion because I had problems, mainly sexual, and I stayed with it because it worked – though not in the way I imagined or wanted.

I was a curious and pragmatic youngster and I thought I'd try religion for myself. After all, that was how I'd come to Marxism. But Marxism, though good at the problems of late capitalism, wasn't good at personal problems, sexual or otherwise, just as it wasn't good at art or intuition.

At that period I had little time for religion. I didn't believe in its mostly pseudo miracles, its confusion of historical truth with mythical truth, and the way religious people had so often burned other religious people or anybody else who dared disagree with them – so like Stalin's gulags.

So why did I go along with it? A question I asked myself frequently and sometimes tried to cheat on. But religion, my own religion, forced me to honesty – albeit reluctantly. One very solid reason was my discovery of *A Year of Grace* by Victor Gollancz. I was mesmerized by the quality and beauty of the people I met in it – their overwhelming generosity of spirit, the beauty of their lives, their courage and their kindness. 'This was the real thing,' I said to myself. They infected me with spirituality like measles. I began to discover my soul, the awesomeness of goodness, and the ugliness of evil – as Marcus Aurelius had done so many centuries ago.

I began to understand what religious people were yammering about. And the outer wrappings of religion were a hoot to boot! All that dressing up and parading and fascination with power (sublimated sex). I enjoyed the flutings of Anglican voices raised to Richard Straussian heights and a battalion of priests co-celebrating mass *en bloc* and marching up and down aisles. It was so much more interesting than those solid lugubrious May Day processions in Red Square. I've always been fascinated by processions and marching around, and I felt impelled by command of God to join them (he must have giggled), just as I'd joined the anarchists, the Kropotkinites, the forces of the Third International, and the Fourth too, the Young Rechabites, and even the Young Britons during my evacuation years.

But back to religion; I had found in my meanderings that something moved in the silences I opened myself up to. Whether it was in me or outside me I didn't know and couldn't know. But these silences were not a blank. They cleansed my judgement and my motives and quietened me. In shorthand, I called them 'Heaven'.

These are the places in which they occurred. Some Anglo-Catholic churches which I began to drop into, not because of their tangled theology and confusing apostolic lines of authority, which meant little to me, but because they seemed to understand what Holiness was; and sitting in them, surrounded by bright pictures of heaven in the colours of childhood sweets, I began to experience it – if not to understand it. It was very sweet! I tried to explain this to Marxist friends, but they thought it drivel and shut their minds against it because it was so disconcerting. I told them to try it, but they never would.

I had experienced that same sweetness when my granny had waved her hands over the Sabbath candles decades before. I began to light Sabbath candles myself and welcome in the angels, whoever or whatever they were, in the company of my two dogs waiting for their dog-chocs. A part of me began to live in another dimension.

This also happened in poorly attended Anglican Evensong and Compline services. They are the least vulgar services I have known, and with Holiness came inner quietness. They were blessedly free from the tangles of Communion services where everyone was having a headache about who could have it and who couldn't and in what kind, by hand or mouth, or what about a blessing for non-believers? What about a blessing for non-believers, indeed!

The sum total was that I now knew that this world wasn't the whole story. There was another dimension and it was very powerful; it was redirecting my awareness and my judgement.

Remembering what you fancy you feel!

An Arab friend of mine gave me his circle of worry beads. I was in a bad state and he said my need was greater than his. Some time afterwards, a novice pressed a rosary into my hands, which I didn't use in the traditional manner – the accompanying prayers seemed so mournful (the dolorous thoughts outnumbering the cheerful ones) – when what I needed was a lift.

However, both sets of beads turned out to be very helpful, though not in the ways their well-meaning donors intended.

When I was having analysis, I had more difficulties with memory than I had expected. Fellow 'analysands' recounted their dreams in original and dreadful detail, and I could remember only something about killing dad in order to make love to ma, which wasn't very original. I was told to keep a pencil and notebook beside my bed and record my dreams, forcing myself to wake up and jot them down. This I found unexpectedly tough and, since my dreams were vivid, original and sensational; upon awakening, I assured myself it didn't matter because I certainly wouldn't forget them – and promptly went back to sleep.

But of course I did forget them, and there went the subject matter for my next session on the couch. My analyst sighed and shook his head. But it helped me if I attached each dream to a bead with a word. My analyst was surprised but pleased at my practical use of piety. As I fingered them, I remembered the exotic attachments.

It was the same with religious experience, with my occasional flashes of enlightenment, with the words that stole into my head while meditating or contemplating, with the heaven I sometimes seemed to touch. I hadn't realized how seemingly fragile they were and how easily forgotten or lost in my seething, overcrowded mind.

It was then I remembered my beads and attached my spiritual experiences to them – one word per bead, just as I had attached my sexual experiences to them for the analyst. These became an integral part of my own scripture. This simple device was nothing new: in the time of Moses, the Hebrews must have had the same problem. 'Tie knots in the corners of your garments,' says the Torah – the Mosaic Law, 'to remember God and his commandments, to remember them and do them.' Jesus, in the Gospels, wears the traditional fringes and knots for remembrance, so he must have faced the same problem.

Certain poems have been a great help in my life. They are the best way to encapsulate the immediacy and strength of spiritual experience. These are my favourites which live in me – my good companions!

François Villon's message as he lay in gaol awaiting sentence, a small-time crook in fifteenth-century Paris. He imagines himself as one of the swaying skeletons hung from a gibbet outside the city walls. This is how he addresses a comfortable bourgeois passer-by:

Brother human beings, who live after us,
Don't harden your hearts against us.
Because if you take pity on us poor chaps

God will take more pity on you
You stare at us now five or six of us, hanging from gibbets.
As for our flesh which we nourished too often,
It's already devoured, it's in bits or dust,
And we're just the remaining bones that have became ashes
    and powder.
Don't laugh at the wrong we did!
Just pray to God that he pardons you along with us!

Nobody knows what happened to Villon. Was he executed? Did he escape from gaol? But his words move me more than any other poem I know. Bertholt Brecht was also drawn to it, for there it is in German translation, a high point, perhaps the highest point of his *Threepenny Opera*.

Another poem is my comforter – 'The Guest' by George Herbert. Alone and 'flu-ridden, I spent Chanukah and Christmas holed up in a German gaststalle (boarding house). I was crying with loneliness and abandonment. Then 'The Guest' surged up in my mind. It is the purest and simplest prayer of English (and Welsh) mysticism, and it changed the way I looked at the world – it began to take away a lot of fear.

Titus Brandsma: 'Before a picture of Jesus in prison' written during the Nazi occupation of the Netherlands. It made me understand the real greatness of Christianity. I felt it.

'Adon olam' simplicity – immanent and transcendent are united and you cannot even see the join. Very simple, very profound.

The cause of tragedy

Our hearts go out to the families of those who die in horrific accidents the technical causes of which we don't know.

But I can say something about other tragedies, tragedies which weren't the result of a failure in our technology, but a failure in our souls. I remember them because in my Jewish New Year sermons about repentance and putting things right I used to tell my congregation how wonderful their tradition was and then I accused them of betraying it. To my surprise they said I didn't make them feel guilty enough, which left me confused – I couldn't do right.

But this message could get under their skin because it's not about how they've let religion down, but how religion can let them down. Examine the news! It's not only wicked unbelievers who are causing trouble in the world but pious ones too – when their piety is mixed with politics.

I think of the Israeli Arabs shot on a peaceful bus, the pious assassins of Rabin and Sadat, the self-sacrificing suicide bombers, the over-zealous Christians in the Yugoslav wars, and the massacre of Muslims at Srebrenica. How can religion go so wrong?

Here's a story. A Jewish congregation was split. Some wanted to stand and chant certain prayers and others to sit and meditate silently. 'Let the ancient tradition of the congregation decide,' said the chairman desperately. But the only one who knew it was in an old-folks' home and going gaga, and a delegation rushed to see him. The chanters put their case, but the confused old boy said, 'Our tradition wasn't quite like that.' The silent sitters then put their case, but he said it wasn't exactly like that either. 'Please remember!' pleaded the delegation, 'because it's mayhem – they're hurling their prayer books at each other.' The old boy suddenly beamed. 'That's it,' he said, 'that was indeed our tradition!'

Fresh traditions are needed to mend the failure in us and lead us to a less violent future. Tradition is a way to God but it is not God.

Chapter 10

God at Work! Getting to Grips with the World

Introduction

In eighteenth-century Poland, a controversy broke out among the Jews. On one side were the ethical legalists and on the other the wayward Mystics. There are many stories about their controversies.

Now the leader of the legalists was the great Rabbi Elijah of Vilna whose academy was famous for its rigorous piety. It is recorded that, in one of his classes, he noticed the students looking not at their books but out of the window.

'What are you looking at?' he asked the first.

'That bird soaring upwards in the air,' came the reply.

'And what were you thinking as you watched it?'

'Of the soul soaring upwards to God,' the student replied.

'Please leave my class,' he told the student. 'You are too poetic to be pious!'

'And what were you thinking?' he asked the other student.

'I was thinking,' came the reply, 'if that bird dropped dead in that hedge between the two farms, which farmer could claim the body?'

'Thank God,' said Rabbi Elijah. 'There is someone here who knows what religion is about!'

During the credit crunch, I needed the Holy Spirit to deal with the problems of this life. What lay beyond would have to wait until I got there.

I also needed the Holy Spirit for the contortions of Middle East politics and in the busy business of economic survival in a dodgy time of dubious banking and climate change.

I did not learn how to connect together this world and the world beyond in libraries or seminaries but in the BBC where, for 40 years, I have been slotting a God-slot into a fast news programme – usually on Monday mornings.

Stock Market blues

I spread out my breakfast paper and read through what my stars foretell and then what the stocks and shares man foretells. He is glum because the Stock Market is having hiccups and the yiddisher mama in me wants to cheer him up with chicken soup. I'm relieved when a fellow rabbi rings. He's preparing for the Jewish High Holy Days in September but he's short-handed, can I help out? Of course – I'm more at home laying up treasure in heaven than treasure on earth.

Actually, when the Stock Market is having hiccups, sermons present few problems, because when the FTSE goes down, spirituality goes up. You intone 'This World is a fleeting cloud, a passing shadow', and the bright business graduates in the congregation nod sagely and sadly. 'Invest yourself in good deeds,' I quote, 'whose interest you enjoy in this life and whose capital awaits you in the world to come.' To retired professionals, this is a prospectus from heaven. 'Don't invest your heart in the things of this world,' I warn, 'because when they break, your heart will break with them.' 'Too true, too true!' they sigh.

If you've lost a lot, then your first practical task is to stop brooding over your losses, so that they don't fester inside you – which isn't easy. A Japanese proverb says that the hardest thing in life is to let go, and it's the bad memories that are hardest to let go, not the good ones.

Here are two seemingly silly ways not to brood. The first is mentally to gift-wrap all your losses, and make God a present of them as it were. They're his now, not yours, so don't think about them any more. The second is to follow this zany advice from the sages – the more you lose, the more you give to charity. This won't make you rich again but will make you feel rich again, because there's always someone poorer than you to whom you can do a good turn.

On a less exalted level, remember there's no such thing as free lunch, and Newton proved, centuries ago, that what goes up must come down. These facts should deter you from blaming everyone except yourself, which is dangerous because that way you could lose not just paper money but your spouse, life partner, or best friend. For poor and rich are really relative terms.

A man sees his mate in a pub gloomily quaffing vintage champagne. 'What's wrong, old chap?' he says. 'My auntie died in May,' answers the man gloomily, 'and left me ten thousand. And then grandpa passed away in October and left me eight thousand.' 'Sorry about them,' says his friend, 'but why so fed up? You've done jolly well.' The man bursts into tears. 'Yes, but we're into October again,' he sobs indignantly, 'and so far – nothing!'

Prayer when the FTSE goes down

When the FTSE goes down, spirituality goes up. When the old securities of jobs for life, mortgages and bank accounts no longer seem so solid, hard-headed business types have been known to consult the Talmud and other religious writings about spiritual investments, some of which are very enticing in a time of massive national debt.

'Invest in good deeds,' say the old rabbis, 'you'll enjoy the interest in this world, and the capital remains intact for you in the world to come.' Free, presumably, from climate change and hyper-inflation.

And if your real estate business collapses on you, then perhaps it's a coded call from God to forsake the things of this world, lead a simpler life and become a priest, pastor, nun, monk or rabbi hard-selling you homes in heaven.

Even my pious peasant granny's primitive monetary policies bear re-examination. She saved her household money under her wig and kept a corner of her precious parlour unplastered as a reminder that here is no abiding city and that one small pogrom could wipe out the labours of a lifetime.

The Stock Market wobbles like a jelly and my savings with it, and not just my savings but my character and soul as well, which shocks me. From being a rather nice guy, I become a rather nasty one. I thought I was made of stronger stuff.

I watch myself getting meaner. I join the rugger scrum round the reduced price shelves at the supermarket, and turn out some memorably awful meals, substituting mousetrap cheese for mozzarella. It tastes like soap, and my guests decline second helpings.

I want to blame everybody except my own greed for my losses – just like a child whining about adults. I get irritable with people around me but stop short, thank God, of picking a row with my friend, who is much more important to my life than numbers on bits of paper.

But what irritates me most is the damage to my pride. Why wasn't I all-knowing? Fortunately I remember the beggars of my childhood, and cheer up. They'd lost the lot, but they never lost their self-esteem.

A clothes manufacturer used to give one of them a sixpence every evening for luck. But one evening he was held up and missed out. At two in the morning he rushed downstairs in panic as the door-bell kept on ringing followed by bangs on the windows. He opened the door, and there stood his beggar! 'Where's my sixpence?' shouted the angry beggar. 'O God,' whimpered the manufacturer, tears of tiredness streaming down his cheek, 'couldn't you wait 'til after breakfast?' 'I don't try to organize your business,' said the beggar grandly, 'so don't try to organize mine!'

I laugh, and life brightens up a bit. I've got enough to eat, a place to sleep, I can afford a budget holiday and, though I'm an OAP, I still work. There are millions in Africa who could live on my leftovers.

But my biggest worry isn't about material things at all – it's this. If my soul wobbles so much over small changes in this life, how is it going to manage the greater change just over the next horizon or two, when my soul will have to pass from the life of this world to the life of the next? At present, it's too wobbly and too attached to worldly things to make it. I'm 80 now and had better firm it up.

Some of you have asked me to pray for your souls at various times – which I've done. Now it's your turn to pray for mine. One good turn deserves another. This is no joke. I'd appreciate it.

Yet another recession

I got sucked into the mini building society stampede. Like a headless chicken, I joined tight-lipped savers outside high-street offices. Some said the government guaranteed £35,000, others £50,000. A helpful Indian lady urged me to get diversified, but I was just a foolish financial lamb who had gone astray – ba ba ba. I felt guilty, adding to the panic, like a rat leaving a sinking ship. After all, I only wanted complete security with high interest like everybody else.

But I couldn't help myself. Memories welled up from childhood, because I was brought up in the shadow of the Great Depression of 1929. I remember dad looking for work, and losing his pride, and the rent man coming to collect what we hadn't got. I shopped for cracked eggs, broken biscuits and yesterday's cakes. I earned ha'pennies crooning, 'Brother, can you spare a dime?'

I returned home angry with myself and my money, and unloaded my worries on my partner. He flinched. I'd worried him and felt sorry for us both. He was older than me, and I'd used him as a scapegoat. In desperation, I prayed to my Friend in High Places, my Whomsoever-Whatsoever, to stick around and help me. 'Don't lose your soul with your savings, Lionel,' he whispered.

It's not difficult to lose both. I saw it happen as a kid peering behind a curtain at hungry miners and stricken refugees. An out-of-work housepainter called Hitler, with a talent for radio, had joined people's bitterness over a lost empire to their panic as their savings and jobs disappeared down a black hole, followed by a vicious hunt for scapegoats.

And then came madness and murder.

I remembered an anecdote of that time and shivered. 'Who's responsible for Germany's misfortunes?' the Nazi asked the Jew. 'The Jews and the bicycle riders!' said the Jew. 'Why the bicycle riders?' asked the startled Nazi. 'Why the Jews?' replied the Jew resignedly.

Whose turn is it to be scapegoat now, I wondered – yours, mine? I shivered again. Play it again, Sam!

If you're fragile and frightened by another recession, give your losses to God so your bitterness won't poison you, and be generous with what you *have* got because 'God loves a cheerful giver', as the hymn says. Don't shove or push, but help those worse off than you, as we did during the Blitz but didn't in 1929. And then we won't lose our souls along with our savings. Who knows? These days could be the happiest days of our lives.

Press 1 for this and 2 for that and 3 for God . . .

Before she died, my mother tearfully asked me to help her with the telephone, which surprised me because, though an awful cook, she prided herself on her office skills. But modern technology had

defeated her, like so many oldies. 'No problem, ma,' I said noncha-
lantly – a bureaucrat with two doctorates! No telephone was going
to mess with me. On my sixth attempt, a pretty voice answered
which spoke but couldn't listen, being recorded not real.

'Press 1 for this and 2 for that,' it said sweetly, 'and 3 for the other
and 4 for something else.' Options 5, 6 and 7 disappeared down the
plughole because I couldn't keep up. With pen and pad, I tried
again. I noted down the options, gambled on 2, and a stern voice
said, 'At an executive meeting. Try next Tuesday.'

'I bet he's at the fish and chipper,' said ma.

The recorded lady then assured me that they treasured my call
but no messages were accepted – and the line went dead.

To seem business efficient while actually being self-protective,
many religious offices, like government or business departments,
now use recordings to replace the old switchboard ladies who listened attentively in their little cubby-holes, guiding the mad, bad,
confused, old or aggrieved through the ecclesiastical maze.

As a student I used to sit by them munching my lunch. Sometimes they left me in charge and I wrestled with frantic enquiries
such as what to do with crematorium ashes or the wedding leftovers
for the choristers. An intellectual wanted fresh faith, an old lady a
husband to cuddle (the fresher the better), a beggar a voucher for a
Sally Army hostel, and a bereaved caller a Jewish cemetery which
would accept a non-Jewish partner alongside. The distraught
enquirers all needed patience – not recordings or theologies or con-
descension.

The switchboard ladies didn't have all the answers of course –
who has? But their kindness eased life's absurdity and pain.

I learned a lot of jokes from them which also eased life's awfulness.

An old man pushes past them into the synagogue demanding to
see the rabbi, who interrupts his supper to see him. 'I've kissed a young
lady,' stammered the greybeard passionately, 'again and again and

again.' 'Recite these prayers!' said the rabbi, wearily. 'I can't,' said the greybeard, 'you see, not being Jewish I can't read Hebrew.' 'Then why tell me your sordid story?' asked the indignant rabbi. 'Because I want to tell everybody,' shouted greybeard, waving his arms ecstatically.

'There's none so queer as folk!' as the telephone ladies used to say. I recommend this Yorkshire adage, whose truth I verified at the switchboard, to high clerics meeting in solemn assembly and to humble folk on summer retreats.

I learned the text of life from working in restaurants as a waiter and a barman, and in the BBC, and doing one-man shows at theatres and, as I've said, at a switchboard.

Suicidal at Christmas

'Be prepared!' as Scouts say – for festival displays are lighting up for Jewish Chanukah, Christmas, and New Year's Eve. Their messages differ, but their fall-out is the same. We are urged to be merry, and to play happy families. But as many have no families, or mislaid them, or their families weren't that happy in the first place, they feel more alone than ever. Some hit the bottle or think about suicide. These practical and tried tips may help, all personally tested.

If you daren't risk depression on your own, what about a hotel Christmas? You can get Bucks Fizz with breakfast in bed and no washing-up, though it doesn't come cheap. Ask about line dancing, and don't be relegated to the table for one beside the swinging kitchen door.

Less expensive are Christmas house parties in retreat centres. Your fellow guests are mainly middle class and middle aged, who pass things politely at table, and there's a chapel where you can natter about your soul. There's a kettle for cocoa, and hot-water bottles, as well as a small bar, but not enough baths en suite. Book early!

Why not create a fresh family out of friends and acquaintances and their attachments. Tell them to bring a dish and/or bottle and help wash up. In return they can pry into your kitchen drawers and cupboards. Allow them to be themselves, merry or miserable – that's the best present of all.

A jolly place to enjoy a festival is a launderette in bedsitter country. We all used to share a feast of fish and chips while watching our smalls whizzing round to saucy comments.

And what about facing a religious festival head-on? One Sabbath eve in winter I was holed up in a foreign hotel with 'flu. I'd read a poem by George Herbert in which Love was his guest. Feeling rather foolish, I croaked out an old Hebrew hymn inviting the angels of the Sabbath to come and keep me company. Well, something came into me, because my jealousy of the people boozing in the bar downstairs drained out of me. I felt tired but quiet. Before I went to sleep I decided to become angelic myself and ring two friends in London lonelier than I was.

You might say this is just imagination stuff, but imagination carries us into a world beyond facts and figures, which becomes fact when we seal it with a generous deed. The rest is bling! Have a big-hearted time!

A not so Holy Land

The Holy Land isn't that holy. Sure, there's a lot of religion, but a lot isn't first quality – it's more concerned with holy places than holy actions, with building walls not bridges, and mixing nationalism with communalism into pious lethal cocktails. It stimulates assassination paranoia and pride as well as heroism, self-sacrifice and creativity. The most obvious thing we outsiders can do is to give to reputable charities which give food and medicines to women, children and oldies caught up in the violence – to stave off disaster.

I haven't been there for over 40 years but the facts haven't changed. Israel has won every war, but every war makes another war more likely. The Arabs can afford to lose wars, Israel can't afford to lose one – it's too small.

Can Israel win a peace? Between the wars there are short opportunities for peace but, if they're not realized by facts as well as words, hatred grows, trust melts away, and the price of peace goes ever higher. One day it will be too high to pay, and we're dangerously near that now.

Over 40 years ago this joke was popular. The American President says to Golda Meir, Prime Minister of Israel, 'What aid can we give you, Golda?' 'Two of your generals,' she says. 'Which ones,' he asks, astounded, 'seeing that your generals are real winners?' 'General Motors and General Electric,' she replies.

But we now know the problem isn't military or economic but fear and mistrust. So religion may be more relevant than technology if it's up to the job. Let's ask God for courage to begin to tackle the basic injustices. The Palestinian refugees with no right of return or restitution. The corresponding rights of Jewish refugees from Arab countries. Jerusalem as the capital of two nations, not one. The illegal settlements and opportunist shifting frontiers. Equal economic opportunities for Palestinians and Israelis.

Let's pray for a new breed of politician who takes responsibility for two peoples, not one, with a vision which might win the hearts of a new generation.

There are some small lights in the darkness of the Holy Land. There's a Jewish, Christian, Muslim village near Jerusalem, and hundreds of thousands of telephone calls between bereaved parents of both sides, to each other. There's a Palestinian Israeli Orchestra, and football teams. Youngsters on both sides want to meet each other at discos – they're curious.

Friends of mine have just come back from Israel attending the birth of a baby. The father made an impromptu speech. 'A baby isn't born with hate. It's society that puts hate in.'

Which means that every baby and every new generation is an opportunity for past mistakes and wrongs not to be repeated.

Turning troubles into treats

What with bombs, murders and strikes, the morning's news is not very good. Some say the old days were nicer, but that's not how I remember it; for we lived in the shadow of one world war followed by a slump, miners' strikes and mass unemployment, while waiting for another war we might not win. We didn't worry about atom bombs but poison gas.

Will this ever change? I don't think so because horror is a quicker fix than contentment. An old building coming down is more fascinating than a new one going up. Great comedies are rarer than great tragedies.

Also the modern recipe for happiness doesn't work. Power, publicity and money deliver comfort possibly, but not happiness. That is inside us and in a different dimension, so society's on the wrong track.

But my job hasn't changed over the years. It's helping you and me get out of bed on a Monday morning and giving us enough spiritual stiffening not to jump back into it. Making us not happy but happier.

Here are my stratagems: use your God-given bodies to chase away the blues. Sing songs which connect you to your inner life. What about that cleansing hymn, 'All that I am, all that I do, all that I'll ever have I offer now to you' or feel frisky singing 'I'd like to teach the world to sing in perfect harmony'. They'll give you your spiritual lift.

Dance a bit like King David. Unlock the tensions in your muscles, if you're up to it. Conga or hokey-cokey to your bathroom. Or what about Yoga? Or pretending you're a bear? Being a child isn't childish but closer to heaven.

Work releases you from the horror movies in your mind, and it's what we're put in this world for. So get going – clear out a drawer, make soup, write a symphony. And give something. Use the morning news to tell you who needs help. If you're broke, give a cuddle, a compliment or a phone call.

My mother was very good at turning troubles into treats. About 50 years ago, her bosses gave her a liquidizer to make them vegetarian lunches. Ma didn't think the blades went round fast enough, and liquidized the top of her finger. She wrapped her hand in a napkin, served the juice, and passed out in the kitchen. When she came to in hospital she was jubilant. 'Lionel,' she whispered, 'it was carrot, not cabbage soup, so the colour didn't give me away.' 'Thank God,' she added piously – and passed out again.

Chapter 11

Ageing, Dying, Death and Heaven

An introduction to ageing

I am no gerontologist or geriatrician or social worker or medic, so I shall rely on my own experience and the experience I gained looking after my elderly mother and aunt, and from visiting in old-folks' homes, hospitals and hospices. I only wish I had listened more and gabbled less. At the time I thought I gabbled to cheer my clients and parishioners – now I know it was to shield me from facing fairly and squarely the problems of ageing.

I meet fellow oldies on the street and in the supermarket where we jostle our baskets and trolleys. Many look sad and cheated. They see old age as a road to nowhere via loneliness and the loss of old friends. I want this book to cheer them; hence the inclusion of oldie jokes where they make or stress a relevant point. When you're bewildered, startled or confused, life can seem like a sadistic joke, but black humour is not sadism.

How did I know ageing was coming on? A girl stands up for me in the Underground; hospital becomes my second home; in love there is less climax but more foreplay; and I receive an official letter telling me that I shall now receive an extra 25p pension per week. I appreciate the thought!

A gay life!

Dear Godseeker,

I'm now going to step cautiously into an ecclesiastical minefield because I've been a gay religious bureaucrat for 40 years, out but not outed, and therefore have scarcity value. My clerical life is told in this book and needs no re-statement. As to my personal life, here is an updating of my story – the two parts of my life (body and soul) are closely intertwined. My partner and I have lived together faithfully for over 25 years. I am 80 and he is 84, and it mostly doesn't seem a decade too much. I don't want to raise more argument, only to add some overlooked aspects of the controversy about people like us. This world and the next, sex and love, body and soul, have to be brought into relationship because they are all God-given and need each other.

For example, there has been much discussion about straight children adopted by gay parents. I've experienced a not exactly comparable situation, but yet with echoes of it. What it was like being the gay and only child of straight parents in an overwhelmingly straight society? A nightmare! The burden of silence, secrecy and lies, and the fear of blackmail and arrest collapsed decent relationships. Many youngsters had breakdowns and some tried suicide. I tried myself. One cleric threw me out. Another told me to go abroad where no one knew me – but I didn't have the fare.

But youngsters now, thank God, get a better reception though, in some places, life imprisonment and execution are returning as in Hitler and Stalin days, and official silence is once again deafening. So why bother about religion?

Because though religion has a lot to learn about sex, sublimation and gender, and that 'one size doesn't fit all', it taught me a lot about spiritual love and that sex isn't the purpose of our life on earth. Also, gay people have their own spiritual needs. You need a lot of God to transform friends into a family and a house into a home. Also, same-sex relationships are a more complex fit physically, socially and psychologically.

Another problem comes with age. Which care homes would accept our Derby and Derby situation? Is there room for us at the inn? We're old, and a civil partnership would be easier for the survivor. We don't want to be excluded from each other's funerals, as has happened.

The first step forward is so simple it needs some godly courage. Gays and believers meeting and listening with the heart to each other's life experience and truth, without dismissive jabs or passing the buck. Some homo humour would help.

Two ancients on holiday sit silently in their car, holding hands and gazing sleepily at the sea, musing as oldies are inclined to do. 'We should get civilly partnered,' said one slowly 'But what partners would want us now?' moaned the other despairingly. God would! He enjoys his oddballs and their healing laughter.

Smart casual but decrepit

The problem! I am still a young person but in an old person's body. I haven't yet caught up with the changes in attitude that old age requires.

Life is a school, say the rabbis, and that is the syllabus – acquiring, giving, giving back. Though I was never pretty, I face the same problem as the Marschallin in the First Act of *Der Rosenkavalier* as she gazes at her face in the mirror and feels the heart-breaking sadness of time passing.

The transition to old age from middle age is as significant as growing up from adolescence to adulthood, and whereas, as I've said, there is an army of counsellors and helpers to assist with the earlier right of passage, there are far, far fewer people who can help or counsel you about your later transition. The name of the game is now not sex but soul, which is more difficult to locate being non-sensible (though not non-sense). But it is also a time for growing – as important a time as any, maybe even the most important.

But there is no need to be over-glum. I tried to commit suicide in my early twenties, but wouldn't do that now. In fact, my seventies were nicer than my sixties, and my sixties nicer than my fifties. I wouldn't wish my teens or twenties on my worst enemies.

I admit straight away that I am lucky. I am comfortable middle; middle class, not rich, but I don't have to worry about food, heating or rent and, though expensive cruises are beyond my touch and designer clothes only come to me via the aforementioned charity shops, I never forget that my grandparents had no pensions and my parents just scraps of pensions, while I am really pensioned (though not as well as most of my colleagues as I don't have an orderly CV). Also some of my choices did not turn out to be as secure as their comforting names suggested. Government pensions are fine if their value isn't fiddled by inflation. Comfort is important but you don't expect your contentment and happiness from others – you have to create it yourself.

The plusses of pensioned old age! I'm free of the rat-race, networking and enthralment to the bitch goddess Success.

Ma's advice to me just before her death: 'What you've done, Lionel, you've done – and the rest is gravy.' What she meant by this sibylline remark is a matter for speculation. I too 'can also wear purple' and so can you. I can permit myself tomato pilchards from the tin and rice pudding likewise. I can be free! But not too sloppy, mind, or the effect will not be smart casual but decrepit.

You might not be agile, but to have got so far in worldly life means that you probably have a store of experience tucked away in the recesses of your mind and soul. I only learned how to keep a relationship going after I was 50. An old friend of mine used to say that the wiles and experience of the old can defeat the optimism and prettiness of the young every time. An overstatement of course – but worth considering.

Learning the new facts of life – the long littleness of it – such as dressing will take you double the time. Journeys will have to be planned like military strategies. Being more dependent, you will have to know who to suborn to your needs and how.

Turning troubles into treats. How to prepare for long waits in hospitals and at security offices. If you have no family, your friends will have to serve instead. Growing old alone for many is a mug's game. How to join up with a partner, spouse or friend, how to make a family out of friends.

Now here is the *important* bit for Godseekers. As this world begins to break down, you have to invest yourself more in another dimension. The Beyond Life is accessible in this world if you make the effort and, though you may have left it a bit late, the sooner you start transferring to it, the more at peace you will feel – not just with ageing but with the greater change of dying.

Get acquainted with that Beyond Life. He/It/She can replace your worldly friends, and there's a lot of contentment and pleasure in contemplation. Go to retreats which examine it.

I read tombstone inscriptions, other people's last thoughts – usually rather cheering and often saucy. I read poems which convince, like 'General William Booth Enters into Heaven' by Vachel Lindsay, Titus Brandsma's meditation poem in prison, the hope of Anne Frank and those like Thérèse of Lisieux who have made something of the apparent 'black hole'. I join the company of François Villon and my granny. What a combination!

So keep spiritual anthologies and guide books by your bed and with you when you travel, like those of Dame Cicely Saunders or *A Book of English Belief* by Joanna Hughes.

If straightforward spiritual reading is not your line, try the same thing mediated through art or music – Rembrandt's heads of old people, for example, or through jokes.

Find yourself a teacher.

You have to transfer your interests from where you have come from to where you are going. This will help you to deal with the odds and ends of your worldly life, such as it is, more pleasurably.

Work to do? Tidy up quarrels that are long past their sell-by date. Make a proper Will – but keep it simple if you can.

Pass on your life experience – too hardly come-by to waste – write it down or record it.

Ageing – the experience

There are many good books which deal with ageing from a medical, psychological, theological, cosmetic or practical standpoint. This is written from within the *experience* of ageing – what I have discovered and recognized as I've crossed the borders of late middle into old age. The minuses are obvious: weak waterworks and dependence, the death of old friends and consequent isolation, living in a smaller pool, and donating to charity shops.

The plusses may not be so obvious – but they are there. Being brought up in a youth culture, I could only see the latter part of life as a decline. But with ageing comes important freedoms: I can be forthright, and I don't have to worry so much about the role-playing which falsifies so much religion. I have ceased to look for the perfect relationship (same interests, same money, same background, etc.), and find that things work out better with a partner who isn't my clone but my complement. The lessons of life and psychotherapy have slowly become part of me and, though late as always, I have begun to know how to live.

For some people, old age comes sharply – it comes with retirement. Being a self-employed person, I only gradually became aware that the goalposts had shifted, that a distant horizon had come closer, and that I no longer had great lumps of time in which to do things. If I wanted to do something, it must be done soon or not at all – in this life at any rate. This has taken a great burden from my back.

I hadn't expected to be busier as I grew older. I thought I would be more reflective, with plenty of time to consider. But this is not so. I am more involved with the small things in life than ever. I have to make notes conscientiously in a special book or diary and then make notes as to where I have put the diary. I have to check up each evening on what my programme is for the next day, realizing that my capacities and stamina are not static but shifting. To my surprise I am more concerned by daily life than ever I was before, and pray for ingenuity.

I find myself more anxious about small things. I think a lot of it is referred anxiety and may really come from my mortality. But I've begun to realize that this part of my life is a period of growth, less jerky but analogous to the time that separated adolescence from adulthood. It is territory that waits to be explored.

Dear OAP Godseeker, you may start reflecting on the changing realities around you. Social judgements now matter less – you begin to see them through the 'wrong' end of the telescope, and another dimension, some call heaven, comes closer. It exerts a stronger attraction on you, rather like gravity, which is also invisible. You may have time, indeed you should find time, to get acquainted with it. There are many ways into it. You can sit in front of a Vermeer in a gallery and let its silence steal into you. You can do the same looking through the tired skin of Rembrandt's old faces to the compassion and experience of this world beneath and see the inner light that shines through the blotchy folds and worn bones.

Some oldies I have known draw faces, some search for pattern and meaning in pure mathematics. Some write poetry or short stories. You should try to locate your spirit and get acquainted with the world that lies beyond the senses. This should help you release your mind from sadistic hells and saccharine heavens, and medieval and apocalyptic nightmares. The sadism and saccharine exist because they are in you. Speak to them; they might be unloved bits of yourself. Meet yourself again as a child – part of you does become childlike, but that does not mean childish. Write a letter to the young person you once were! Oldies do start to feel young again and are often closer to young people in attitude and outlook.

The spiritual problem we have to address is giving up or detachment. Whatever we receive, we eventually have to give up or give back. The former giving is charity, the latter is detachment.

Dying may turn out to be a pleasurable experience. You/we are lucky. Many pains are now overcome by modern drugs, which is why they have such nice names such as morphine and heroine. We can now exit on a high. Many dying people meet a 'dead' friend or relation who comes to meet them and guides them across the borderline between the life of this world and whatever life lies beyond it.

To get acquainted with the journey, one or two hurried minutes with a minister on a hurried pastoral visit are inadequate. Sign up for a retreat, a comfortable one, and see where it leads. Your life experience should help you separate honesty from wish fulfilment, hype and manipulation. Many older people join Friends' Associations at hospitals. The experience doesn't terrify – it takes away the strangeness.

Old, grey and gay

Well, as an old, grey and gay clergyman, I feel for my gay colleagues of all faiths, especially the closeted ones. Some risk death, many are denied ordinary home life and companionship. Ecclesiastical parties worry about their own theological hurts: I understand and sympathize, but concern is also needed for the daily life hurts that hardworking gay clergy endure. There are more such than people realize, and their experience has helped other excluded minorities and lonely oddballs, the kind that Jesus helped but religions find irritating.

What can gays give and receive from official religion practically? Gays are a mixed lot, like heteros, but they're often realistic about people's love needs. And though selfish sex can become irresponsible and obsessive, love's the way along which most heteros and homos lead their partners towards commitment and some happiness. Gays can be good at friendship. In families, they make good aunts and uncles, and many straight old people join gay congregations because the affection in them bridges sex and age.

Some stern clerical expressions worry me. They look so unloving when they diatribe and denounce. A little gaiety in the old sense might do them a power of good. Now gays are good at kisses and cuddles. Ah! If only catties and proties could cuddle each other on the Falls Road and a black Jew plonk a kiss on a startled racialist, they might break the mould.

In return, the rituals of religion could structure gay people's lives and sanctify their bedsits into homes. Religion could give them a family of faith. It could help them sublimate some sexual energy into spiritual energy and avoid the numbers game.

I visit a gay, very sick oldie. He whispers a story to me about three mothers. One said, 'My daughter gave us a new Michael Angelo for our patio', and the second said, 'My son paid for my year's non-stop cruise round the world.' 'Mine's gay,' said the third proudly, 'and goes from analyst to analyst only talking about me, his mummy.'

How kind of him to cheer me up. I blew him impromptu kisses. May God fulfil our various gifts and natures for good!

Getting acquainted with death

One of the advantages of regular traditional religion is that death doesn't come as a surprise: the mortality of your body is taken as a matter of course – it is memorialized, prayed over and rehearsed throughout the liturgical year. So you have time to absorb the idea of it before you face the shock of it. 'Be prepared' was the slogan of the Scouts – useful advice.

There is no satisfactory way of proving life before life or death after life. It is worth noting that you can never know death or the life of any world or dimension beyond it. You can know dying but not death – you cannot know a negation. Both Before Life and Beyond Life are beyond the dimensions of time and space. I can intuit and feel: but I cannot grasp or prove.

I have made no investigations into such matters: this life has been problem enough – I have never attended a séance or tried to evaluate near-death experiences.

I don't think death is the end or a total annihilation, not just because I would like it so but because this is the way my life and religious experience have led me.

My preparation for death began in childhood. In the cramped conditions of London's poor East End, where the elderly died at home attended by their families, there usually wasn't money to pay for nurses, only for occasional visits by the doctor in emergencies. I didn't like knowing that granny was dying in the room above me and I was worried when I took food to her, but the family took it as normal, so I did the same. I was complimented on being a real man doing what real Jewish men had to do, which made me proud. I don't remember a real rabbi ever coming to our humble home, just some men from the little house synagogue round the corner immediately before and after death. Dad led the prayers and ma's elder sister lit the memorial candle, deputizing for my uncle who was in hospital with TB.

As a child I considered my own death quite seriously. As the refugees from Nazi Germany arrived, I listened to friends and family talking about it while preparing parcels to welcome and comfort the newcomers. They tried to cheer me up by telling me that such things couldn't happen here, but I didn't believe them because they didn't believe it themselves. Mosley was marching in the streets nearby and Hitler seemed to have the luck of the devil. Mentally I prepared myself for an invasion. Being poor and without influence, how could we get out? And if we got out, where would we go, who would take us in? There had been a lot of anti-Semitism around before the Second World War, and no one wanted more poor uncouth market Jews. I decided I would fight to the end and make as much trouble for the invaders as I could (I was no pacifist), and then expire with honour and not in a gas chamber. I met a non-Jewish farmer at a market who told me he had a gun and was going to do the same thing. We would do it together. It was wonderful having a comrade who didn't act, or pretend or run to Hollywood for false comfort. I was a pragmatic child.

So at an early age I knew where I was going and accepted it. This preparation has stood me in good stead. I am still not good with pain, but death doesn't worry me. This is so for many Jews – after all, death is only a matter of time and the condition of our existence. 'Without our consent we are born and without our consent we die,' said the rabbis.

I kept an open mind about what happens after death. I decided early on that God, if he existed, had more explaining to do than I did, which is another Jewish characteristic.

I'm pleased that I learned the facts of life and death so early. It saved me from the torment of a young man (about sixteen or seventeen years old) whom I was sent to comfort when I was an unprepared unskilled student rabbi. He was in a nursing home, alone in a private suite going nuts with anger, grief and bewilderment. I was given strict instructions not to mention the 'D' word to him or to discuss it. I quickly realized that he knew of his approaching death as well as I did, and wanted some help to face up to whatever he had to face up to – to cry out, to sob, or to curse. I told the local rabbi who thanked me for my time and trouble, but dispensed with my services. A faith healer took my place; I never found out what happened.

Dear Godseeker, I am now more experienced and articulate. I have often thought about him, and this is what I would like to tell him and you over 50 years on.

Don't be overcome by death. You can never experience it – only dying. You can only experience life, whether it is the life of this world or whatever life exists beyond the dimensions of space and time, which is almost beyond my intuition or imagination.

One experience helped me – a confused one. But the lessons I have learned from it have stayed with me and supported me (for good) for many years. I can only set out what happened. Physically it happened in Venice where my then partner and I had gone to try and recreate the romance of our early years together. I quickly realized that this was the last holiday we would take together. The grief was overwhelming because parting is also a kind of death. We were both very English and subdued, but inside me and inside him too I think there was the same tangle of anger, grief and bewilderment as within the young chap I have just mentioned – also an icy loneliness. It is better to have someone to quarrel with than no one to respond at all, only one's echo.

My friend – if he was still my friend – went off to a café, and I wandered off into a chapel near the Rialto. I knew that something like this had been going to happen for years, but I was still unprepared for the violence of my feelings. Then Fred, my inner voice, started up. 'Lionel,' it said, or I made it say. 'In this world you can only get gleams of love, but one day you'll get the real thing – so don't get too upset.' I was sure the voice meant that one day I would meet the Being I had been talking to, chatting to, and arguing with since experiencing the 'emptiness' in the silent synagogue or reality turning inside out at that Quaker meeting. If I hung on for dear life to my Friend in High Places, perhaps the world would turn inside out for me. Not this time in a religious meeting but in a very secular life.

Well, we went back to London, gradually cutting off from each other, quarrelling fiercely about how we would divide our home and the junk that a sentimental couple gathers. While we debated the ownership of a knobbly Sicilian wine jug and when the debate was turning very nasty, the voice that spoke in the Rialto Chapel took on a puckish shape and appeared to me, only now outside the face of my one-time partner and erstwhile friend. When it winked I burst into laughter and suggested that this row was most unprofitable for both of us. 'Let's go to the pub at the corner and toss a coin for every article as it comes to mind.' 'Lionel, that's the most sensible thing you've said for years,' he said. So we did, we had a drink, several drinks, and parted as friends, not partners and lovers.

You need a lot of spirituality to make a good divorce, much more so than you need for a good marriage. In the latter your craving body and the approval of society do most of the work for you. In the former when you cry you cry alone – except of course for Fred.

It was only later when visiting hospitals where patients wanted to know if I thought death was the end that I could say truthfully and fairly honestly that I was pretty sure it wasn't. I was going to meet the voice I'd been talking to for most of my life – a sound old rabbinic hope echoed by St Paul in the New Testament. One of the patients asked me what I thought God would say to me at that meeting. I told him that I'd once asked my teacher the same thing (his name was Joseph Weiss and he taught us cabalah). He had replied, 'God will show you the bad you did and its consequences and that will be your hell, and then he will show you the good you did and its consequences and that will be your heaven.' Then God will say, 'Lionel, you did just as I expected, no better, no worse. And now everything is prepared for the feast!'

I've always thought something like that would happen, but now I trust it enough to share my hope with others. Death, as the rabbis said, can be compared to a ritual bath that cleanses away our sins. It's a going home, not an exercise in cosmic sadism.

I know there is no way of proving any of this empirically – but there is no way of disproving it either. And it is not a belief that has come to me out of thin air; I go along with it because it accords with my limited life and religious experience. I've learned over the years that when I face a problem squarely and call on Fred for courage, whether its stage-fright before going on in a theatre or taking an exam I think I might fail, the problem turns inside out and becomes an opportunity.

I don't like dodging the experiences that life throws up at me. There are occasions of course when I might have to, for example turning off my life-support machine. I don't have to be a guinea pig to provide a statistic for the medical profession. But I hope all this will be my decision and not that of any interventionist over-confident cleric or medic.

This has been confirmed by meditations in the Departure lounges of airports when returning home. You make yourself as comfortable as you can, you make acquaintances, and then you go off, but not at a time of your own choosing, to the next stage of your journey home. This world has never felt like home to me.

It feels like a staging post, though I've had some very good times in it.

There are other experiences of course which are almost too obvious to mention: I refer you to some that I have already mentioned in previous chapters.

From the Mystics I've learned that if you trust and lean on nothing, that Nothing can support you, and that if you come to a blank wall, there is somewhere a door specially meant for you and that a light shines even in darkness.

Heaven

There is a rabbinic story about heaven; there is a rabbinic story about everything, but this is an important one.

An impetuous young rabbi asks God to let him see what happens to the righteous in heaven. God grants his prayer. The young rabbi sees a group of old rabbis sitting around a table, studying and discussing the legal problems of the Talmud. The young rabbi is puzzled and discontented. 'Why,' he said, 'that's what they do all the time on earth – what's interesting in that?' God turns on him. 'Don't you realize,' he said, 'the rabbis aren't in heaven – heaven is in the rabbis?'

It is not necessary to die first in order to witness heaven or even to become part of it. As Simone Weil said, even in this life it works on us like gravity, attracting us to itself. Sometimes it reveals itself to us as a free gift, and sometimes we have to invoke its presence. Its presence is all around us, though at first we do not see it because we are not sure what we are looking for. We may be looking for a hedonist heaven or a kitsch heaven or some private power fantasy dressed up in rituals, or some other 'heavenly' ego gratification.

I first became aware of heaven at a boring bridge party. I was sitting it out, kibitzing, watching the four players. A young married couple were playing an older married couple. The young man had declared a small slam and was triumphantly gathering his tricks in. He looked up proudly to his partner, his wife sitting opposite him, as he made their bid. But there was no joy on her face. She wasn't congratulating him. Instead she mouthed at him, 'You bloody fool!' Naturally he looked upset and I moved away because whatever was going on was embarrassing and not meant for snoopers. Nevertheless I was intrigued and later on asked our hostess what it was all about.

The situation was so simple I should have worked it out for myself: the older man was the employer of the younger man. Therefore in the two-dimensional world of cards, the younger man had indeed won but, in the three-dimensional world of company cars, expense account holidays and company bonuses, he had lost, as his wife well knew. A defeat in the two-dimensional world of cards would have served him better in the more inclusive three-dimensional 'real' world.

Pondering that game and drinking a sherry, I was enlightened. I realized that there was an even greater, more inclusive reality beyond the three-dimensional reality – a spiritual one concerned with the successes and disasters of souls. All the realities were stacked inside each other like Russian Babushka dolls. You can win in the three-dimensional reality of money and business, yet lose your soul in the more inclusive fourth dimension which encloses it. Perhaps there are even more realities and dimensions beyond that, and we creatures are not innocent enough or perceptive enough to be aware of them. Mystics certainly hint at them and some claim to know them.

Once I had a framework of understanding and some idea of what I was looking for, I began to see heaven all over the place, and some of the places were very unexpected. Once again I returned to the rabbis of the Talmud and my cabalist, 'Heaven happens whenever something is done for its own sake.'

Dear Godseeker, you don't have to wait for heaven to happen, any unselfish action is an invitation for heaven to be present. You can often tell its presence by an inner glow which stays with you for a short time, often only seconds, and then disappears like a dream you can't remember but know was important.

But it is the real thing, and such seconds need consideration and meditation. Some people record them in a notebook. Some God-seekers compare their experiences of heaven with those of other Godseekers. For some, they are such private, intimate moments that they are only for themselves or perhaps for those they love. I am not a very private person, and here is a selection of ones I have experienced or witnessed which stay with me and help me to remember my heavenly home from which I came and to which I shall return.

There was a woman I met in a park who assured me she had never had a religious experience but, yes, something did happen to her at the supermarket. At the check-out the lady in front of her had muddled her credit cards and the check-out girl was having hysterics trying to sort out the muddle. The angry man in the queue behind her was prodding her in the backside with his trolley to show his annoyance. The woman said, 'I was just about to join in the row and tell them what I thought about them, when I burst out laughing. I sorted out the old dear's cards, pacified the check-out girl and even waved my bum about a bit to give the macho male behind me a better target for his trolley. Now what was all that about?' she said. 'You had a moment of grace, dear,' I said, 'don't forget it!'

And then when I was taken to hospital in an ambulance I was put in a ward of old men. That night I was ill with a tummy upset and I was sick all the way to the bathroom. Having a temperature and not being able to think clearly, I went down on all fours in the darkness trying to clean up the smelly mess with my handkerchiefs and bits of paper – feeling guilty and responsible. Then a voice whispered beside me in the darkness, 'Don't worry mate, I'll help you.' The man in the next bed, ten years older than I was, had slid out of his bed and was on all fours trying to help me. Then a nurse discovered us and tactfully put us back in bed and brought out a bucket and a mop. I was overwhelmed by my fellow patient's kindness. Would I have done the same for him, I wondered? I wasn't sure – probably not.

But I might now because the presence of heaven was in what he did. It has a bead on my broken rosary and belongs to that fourth dimension I thought about after the bridge game.

Such happenings may seem small, but they are very powerful and can change the trajectory of a Godseeker's life for ever!

Be British beyond life!

There's been an orgy of icon bashing, some of it justified but some of it working off the anger left over from the credit crunch and the decline of the West, of which we are a part.

MPs, rich bankers, poor immigrants and celebrities have all been clobbered. Continental friends tell me, 'Don't take your British self-disparagement too heavy, dear.' And I won't – I'll remember instead British institutions that are part of a pastor's weekly round and which make this country one of the best: our charity shops, friendship clubs, voluntary organizations, Macmillan nurses, and, our best contribution to Europe since the Second World War, the hospices for people beyond ordinary curative care inspired by Dame Cicely Saunders. The gentle honesty of hospices frees me from platitudes. So, when patients or relatives ask me if there's an afterlife, they get the truth without frills. For me, death isn't the end, and I believe in a beyond life but not an afterlife because, when we die, time and space die with us so there is no after or before. That beyond life is not so mysterious – we can enjoy a foretaste of it in this life. If, for example, we do something generous for the sake of heaven, heaven happens. You can tell it by the telltale glow it leaves in you. You've done good – you feel good.

I feel that same glow in me reflecting the light of the Sabbath candles in my kitchen. Also at Anglican Compline in almost empty churches – in Quaker quiet – in Carmelite silences – and in cemeteries when those I've loved speak in me. Even at parties when a bit of me moves out of me and looks down on us all with compassion.

This beyond life is my heaven, home and destination.

Some call it conscience: for me it's a friend with a human face as it were, my soul, my guardian angel, my whatever. For 60 years it has led me into common and uncommon sense.

Try it yourself!

A birthday present

I have just reached fourscore years. My home was already full of the detritus of other people's lives garnered from charity shops, and there was no point in adding more, seeing that all the bits would soon have to return from whence they came, and it would be the turn of my life to be remaindered. But that would be a few years yet.

I told friends to forget about presents. A prayer would be helpful – at least I think so, though I'm not sure prayer changes things in quite that way. They could also put some coins in a charity box. Jim is going to give me a ring. I will give myself a custard tart, and my creator has given me Parkinson's.

And this makes a very fitting way to end this book. For, even if I survive Parkinson's disease, something is bound to get me sooner or later – and probably sooner – and without my consent, as the Talmud says.

To my surprise I wasn't very upset on hearing the doctor's report. I had had a happy marriage, friendship or partnership (whatever you like to call it) so life didn't owe me anything, and there was not so much anger or grievance stored up in me. Perhaps I had done the world just as I had done being a religious bureaucrat, and it was time to move on. So, after a few flutterings in my tummy, I managed to absorb it. I wasn't that frightened of death, but I do not like pain. Fortunately, a few months before, I had been given a shot of diamorphine in hospital Casualty and it was bliss! What a nice way to exit!

What helped me was a line from St Thérèse of Lisieux's 'Last Conversations'. I had always been curious about her, though I didn't exactly take to her. But this thought was important. 'It is not Death that takes us from this world but our Creator, God.' This made death purposive, and fitted in with the 'future meeting' message I'd had in the chapel near the Rialto as my previous partner and I were parting. It also fitted in with the light over the altar in the Royal Free Hospital chapel which seemed to sparkle joyously as I stared at it. A church chappie had sent me a rather lugubrious letter about my chances in the great beyond. I couldn't help feeling a bit vulnerable in my situation, but the sparkle of that light danced away death fears.

This brush with mortality had consequences in my daily living, as Freud had said it would: 'You can't live properly until you know how to die.' His message was very much like that of St Thérèse, though they never knew each other, and probably wouldn't have approved of each other.

Now is the time, dear Godseeker, when you will wish me the traditional Jewish comfort words: 'May you live 'till one hundred and twenty, Rabbi Blue.' To which I reply, 'And the same to you.'

It's a nice thought, but I won't make it. Sorry!

Who's Who and What's What

Auden W. H. (1907–73)
Anglo-American poet, Marxist, Vedantist then Anglican. He wrote 'In Memory of Sigmund Freud'.

Baeck, Rabbi Leo (1873–1956)
Twentieth-century German Chief Rabbi in the Hitler time. Scholar, theologian and leader of Progressive Judaism – survived Theresienstadt Concentration Camp.

Bar Mitzvah
Confirmation ceremony for Jewish boys when, at thirteen, they are recognized as men in Jewish ritual and law. They read the weekly portion from the Scroll of the Law in public.

Beatrice
Spiritual love of Dante's life in *Divine Comedy*. He saw her only once and never spoke to her – see Dante.

Bede, The Venerable (*c.* 672–735)
Monk at the Northumbrian monastery of Saint Peter at Monkwearmouth (Sunderland). His most famous work was *Historia*

ecclesiastica gentis Anglorum (*The Ecclesiastical History of the English People*). 'The Father of English History.'

Blake, William (1757–1827)
English contemplative, poet, Mystic and prophet.

Boëthius (c. 480–525)
Christian philosopher when Roman Empire collapsed. Executed by Gothic King. While in prison, wrote *The Consolation of Philosophy*.

Booth, William (1829–1912)
Founder and first General of the Salvation Army, 1865, an evangelical organization with a military style but no weaponry. Special concern with humanitarian aid, the poor and the rejected especially.

Brandsma, Titus (1881–1942)
Dutch Carmelite priest opposed to Nazism. Arrested during the occupation of Holland. In prison, wrote on the picture of Jesus hanging in his cell. Died in Dachau and later canonized as Saint.

Brecht, Bertholt (1898–1956)
Author of *The Threepenny Opera*, he was a Marxist German poet, playwright and theatre director.

Brompton Oratory
Brompton Road, Kensington, London SW3. Founded by Cardinal Newman.

Buber, Martin (1878–1965)
Austrian-born Jewish philosopher. Scholar and interpreter of Jewish East European mysticism and piety (Chassidism).

Buddha Supreme Buddha (*c.* 563 BCE–483 BCE)
Spiritual teacher from India who founded Buddhism.

Bunyan, John (1628–88)
Baptist, tinker, writer and preacher. He was arrested after the Restoration (Charles II). *Pilgrim's Progress* was written while he was in prison.

Butler, Josephine (1828–1906)
Feminist especially concerned with the welfare of prostitutes. There is a window dedicated to her memory in Liverpool Cathedral.

Capuchin Friars
Catholic Friars – an offshoot of the Franciscans.

Carter, Sydney (1915–2004)
English hymnwriter, poet and storyteller – served with the Friends' Ambulance Unit during the Second World War.

Chassidic Rabbis
Polish mystical rabbis. Martin Buber collected their sayings, stories and parables from the eighteenth and nineteenth centuries.

Dante, Alighieri (1265–1321)
Italian poet of the Middle Ages. *The Divine Comedy* tells of Dante's visionary Easter journey through Purgatory, Hell and Heaven, lasting from the night before Good Friday to the Wednesday after Easter in the spring of 1300.

Dawkins, Professor Richard (1941–)
Atheist, controversialist – against religion – science should replace it. Wrote *The God Delusion*.

De Mello, Fr Anthony (1931–87)
Jesuit priest and psychotherapist – widely known for his books on spirituality and outstanding spiritual anthologies.

Elijah, Rabbi Abraham ben Elijah of Vilna (1750–1808)
Jewish Talmudist who lived in Lithuania. A Talmudic teacher and leader of the Jewish community and opponent of Chassidism.

Frank, Anne (1929–44)
Jewish girl born in Germany – fled to Amsterdam in 1933 where she was hidden with her family during the Nazi occupation of Holland. Betrayed – she died of typhus in Belsen in 1945. *The Diary of Anne Frank* was written while she was in hiding and published posthumously.

Freud, Sigmund (1856–1939)
The founder and pioneer of psycho-analysis and teaching on sexuality. Also the significance of dreams, the subconscious and transference. Fled from Vienna – died in London.

Friedlander, Rabbi Albert (1927–2004)
Born in Berlin and studied in America – he was a liberal, scholar, teacher and writer. Director of the Leo Baeck College in London; he wrote a biography of Leo Baeck.

Gollancz, Victor (1893–1967)
Born in Hungary and became an influential British publisher combatting Nazism. Compiler of *A Year of Grace*, his spiritual anthology.

Greengross, Dr Wendy
Counsellor, psychotherapist, teacher, author and agony aunt.

Gryn, Rabbi Hugo (1930–96)
Reform rabbi who was a popular broadcaster and a leading voice in interfaith dialogue in Britain. Born in Czechoslovakia, childhood in Auschwitz.

Harries, Richard Douglas; Baron Harries of Pentregarth (1936–)
41st Bishop of Oxford from 1987 to 2006. Since 2008, he has been the Gresham Professor of Divinity. Now in the House of Lords.

Herbert, George (1593–1633)
'The Guest'. Anglican priest of Welsh origin. Religious, mystical poet, pastor and hymnwriter.

Hillesum, Esther 'Etty' (1914–43)
Young Jewish writer and Mystic whose letters and diaries describe life in Holland under Nazi occupation. Died in Auschwitz.

Hirschfeld, Magnus (1868–1935)
German Jewish doctor and early advocate of gay rights.

Hughes, Joanna Mary
Author of *A Book of English Belief*. Educated at Somerville College, Oxford.

Joyce, James (1882–1941)
Greatest modern Irish writer. Complex and sometimes seemingly obscure.

Julian of Norwich (*c.* 1342–*c.*1416)
English Mystic, anchoress and contemplative in Norwich. Recorded her visions after illness – *Sixteen Revelations of Divine Love*. Met Margery Kempe.

Jung, Carl Gustav (1875–1961)
Analytical psychiatrist who separated from Freud, believing that human psyche is by nature religious. Attracted to Mysticism – Eastern and Western.

Kempe, Margery (Burnham) (*c.* 1373)
English Mystic, married with fourteen children, attracted to charitable works and travel. Honest autobiography details her life and pilgrimages. 'Patron Saint of Package Tours'!

Kerouac, Jack (1922–69)
The Dharma Bums. American novelist of the Beat Generation – influenced by Buddhism.

Kropotkin, Prince Peter (1842–1921)
Zoologist, traveller, Russian idealist and anarchist. He stressed the co-operation of species.

Levi, Primo Michele (1919–87)
Jewish–Italian scientist and writer. He wrote *If This Is a Man* (published in the USA as *Survival in Auschwitz*), his account of the year he spent as a prisoner in Auschwitz, which led eventually to his rejection of religion and eventual suicide.

Leviathan
Sea monster referred to in the Tenach (Old Testament).

Lindsay, Vachel (1879–1931)
American poet whose verses can be chanted. Wrote 'General William Booth Enters into Heaven'.

Littman, Dr Ellen
Biblical scholar, educated in Berlin, and taught at the Leo Baeck
College in London.

**Longford, Lord Francis Aungier Pakenham; 7th Earl of Longford
(1905–2001)**
Politician, Labour Minister and social reformer. Advocate of Mother
Teresa of Calcutta and Simone Weil.

Marcus Aurelius (121–180)
Roman Emperor and Stoic philosopher. His *Meditations* affirm
duty, self-honesty and practical ethics.

Marshall, Fr Gordian OP (Order of Preachers) (1938–2007)
Dominican involved with inter-faith dialogue. Honest and straightforward Scot.

Marx, Karl Heinrich (1818–83)
Economist, philosopher and political theorist. Founder of Commu-
nism. Worked with Engels on *Das Kapital*.

Masoretic Text (MT) of the Tenach (OT)
Authoritative Hebrew and Aramaic text of Tenach (Old Testament).
Authority supported by the Dead Sea Scrolls which are the basis of
the modern translations.

Mosley, Oswald (1896–1980)
Leader of the British Union of Fascists.

Mystic/Mysticism
Communion with and awareness of an ultimate reality, or God,
through direct experience. Also concerned with the origin of evil.

New Statesman
Weekly current affairs magazine.

New Testament: Salome (*c.* 14–62)
Daughter of Herodias – caused the death of John the Baptist.

Nietzsche, Friedrich Wilhelm (1844–1900)
German philosopher, critical of religion and contemporary. Wrote *Death of God* and *Thus Spake Zarathustre.*

Old Testament: Apocrypha (not Tenach)
Maccabees: Victorious against the Greek Kingdom of Antiochus. Ruled from 164 BC to 631 BC.

Old Testament: Tenach
Abraham: Father of a Multitude (Jacob – Judaism and Christianity; Ishmael – Islam). Story told in Genesis.

Amnon: son of David – raped Tamar his half-sister, and then hated her.

Ecclesiastes: Atrributed to Solomon – unlikely. Its wisdom is different from the book of Proverbs with a possible Sadducee influence.

Elijah: Ninth-century BC prophet in Israel. Traditional herald of the future Messiah.

Exodus: The story of the flight and escape of the Israelites from the Egyptians by the crossing of the Red Sea.

Habakkuk: Minor prophet – minor not because he was less important but because his book is shorter than, say, Isaiah or Jeremiah.

Jeremiah: A major Hebrew prophet. Traditionally also the author of Lamentations.

Passover
Festival commemorating the liberation of the Children of Israel from Egypt and the crossing of the Red Sea.

Pietism
Movement of piety and religious zeal – genuine or superficial.

Quakers
Religious Society of Friends. Prominent against the slave trade and for the rights of women, prisoners and gays.

Ravensbrück
Notorious Nazi concentration camp for women in north Germany

Reconquista (Recapturing) (710–1492)
The retaking and reconverting of the Iberian Peninsula from the Muslims by various Christian kingdoms.

Reich, Wilhelm (1897–1957)
Radical psychiatrist and analyst. Pupil of Freud but they then parted company. Sexual liberation.

Ridler, Anne (1912–2001)
British poet, Anglican, honest personal religious thinking.

Rossetti, Dante Gabriel (1828–82)
English poet, artist and illustrator. Founder of the Pre-Raphaelite Brotherhood.

Saint Augustine of Hippo (354–430)
North African with enormous influence on Christian thought – some of it controversial.

Saint Edith Stein (1891–1942)

German Jewess. Became Roman Cahtolic and joined the Discalced Carmelites. Arrested in Holland and gassed in Auschwitz. Philosopher and martyr.

Saint Francis of Assisi (*c.* 1181–1226)

Founder of the Franciscan Friars – love of poverty, nature and animals.

Saint John of the Cross (1542–91)

Reformer – founder of the Discalced Carmelites. A Mystic, poet and adviser and confessor of Teresa of Ávila.

Saint Teresa of Ávila (1515–82)

Mystic, reformer of the Carmelite Order, writer, leading spiritual light of the counter-reformation. Named a 'Doctor of the Church'.

Saint Thérèse of Lisieux (1873–97)

French Carmelite, 'The Little Flower'. Teacher of the 'little way' in *The Story of a Soul* which had enormous influence.

Saint Thomas Aquinas (1225–74)

Dominican whose thoughts have been basic to Christianity since the Middle Ages. Scholasticism.

Saunders, Dame Cicely Mary (1918–2005)

Prominent Anglican nurse, physician and writer. She helped the dying and terminally ill end their lives in the most comfortable ways possible. She is best known for her role in the birth of the hospice movement, emphasizing the importance of palliative care in modern medicine.

Shepard, Leslie (1917–2004)
Reichian analyst, then Vedantist. Folklorist.

Sisters of Sion (Sisters of Our Lady of Sion)
We are called to witness by our life to God's faithful love for the Jewish people. Our call implies that our apostolic life is characterized by a threefold commitment: to the Church, to the Jewish people, and to a world of justice, peace and love. Whatever task we are engaged in, we are called to integrate in some way these three dimensions of our apostolic commitment.

Spencer, Stanley (1891–1959)
English painter – much of his greatest work depicts biblical scenes, from miracles to the crucifixion, happening not in the Holy Land, but in Cookham (Berkshire).

Talmud (second to fifth centuries)
Books of rabbinic discussion in Palestinian and Babylonian academies before and after failed revolts against Rome. The foundation and basis of Rabbinic Judaism.

Tracy, Honor (1913–89)
Perceptive writer on Ireland and Britain. Travel writer in Ireland and Spain. Wrote humorous, astringent novels.

Trotsky, Leon (1879–1940)
Trotskyism. Revolutionary Marxist; lost out to Stalin in Russian political struggles; internationalist.

Vanderzyl, Rabbi Dr Wernher
Educated in Berlin and founder of the Leo Baeck College.

Vedanta
Hindu school of philosophy, stressing self-knowledge, i.e. knowing our own (divine) nature. Spread in Britain and America by Swami Vivekananda.

Virgil (first century BC)
Greatest Latin poet – also guide figure to Dante.

Von der Heydt, Baroness Vera (1899–1996)
German of part Jewish origin. Refugee in Britain during the Nazi times. A leading Jungian analyst. Roman Catholic convert.

Weil, Simone (1909–43)
French–Jewish upper-middle-class background. Marxist who turned to spirituality and modern mysticism. Wrote *Waiting on God* and *Affliction and the Love of God* and *Gateway to God*. Died near London while working for General de Gaulle.

Weiss, Joseph
Hebrew University, London University, Scholar of Chassidism.

Williams, Fr Harry CR (1919–2006)
Member of the Anglican Community of the Resurrection at Mirfield, West Yorkshire. Priest, teacher and monk. An outstanding Anglican theologian and spiritual writer of his day.